Waves of Glory

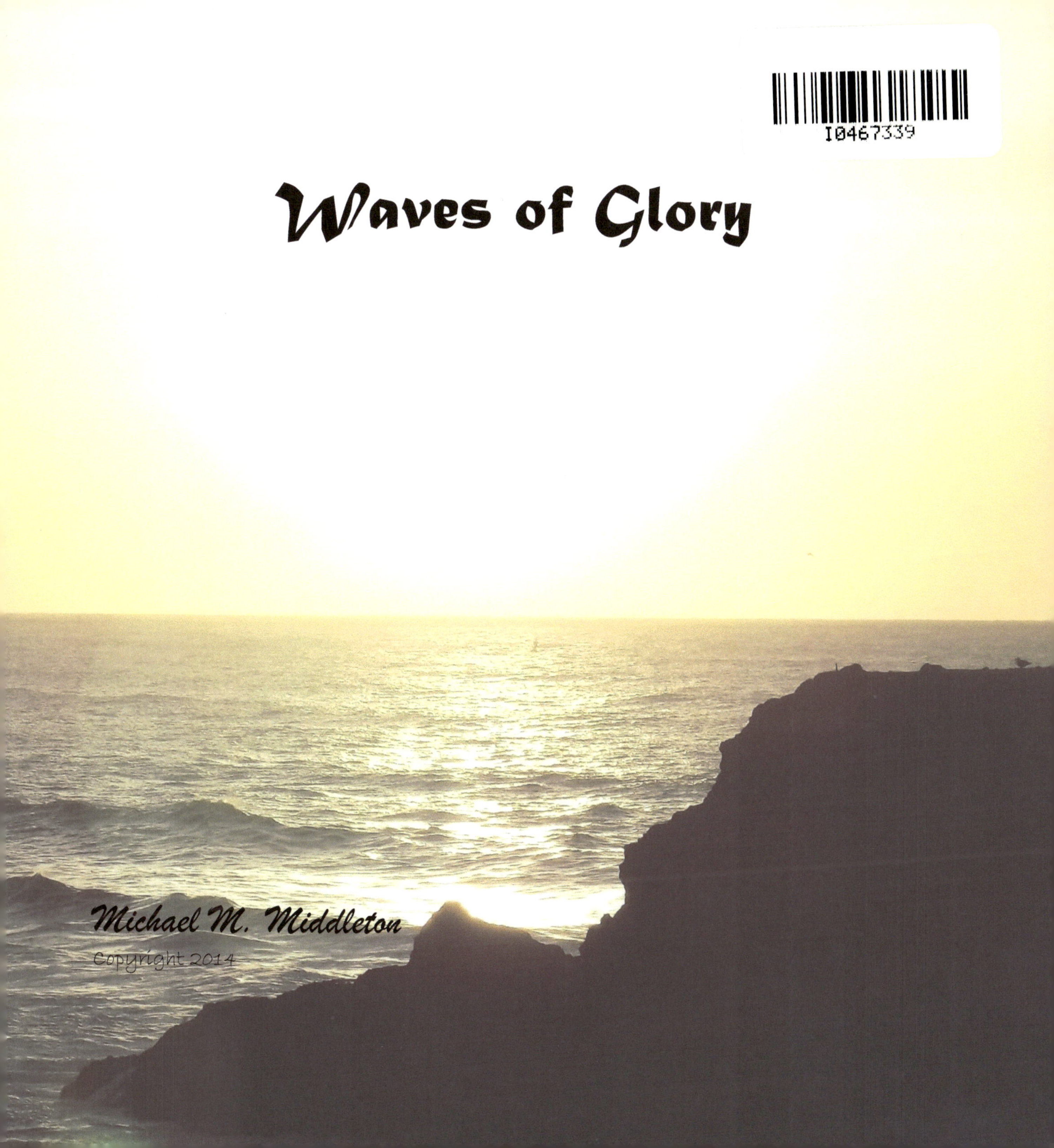

Michael M. Middleton

"Books are a uniquely portable magic."

Stephen King

This work benefits the ministry of Faith Harvest Helpers. Please see a brief introduction to this unique and vital ministry of YWAM at the conclusion.

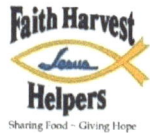

Waves of Glory

In the distance I hear the rolling waves beckoning, calling me home…
Swallowed up, joyfully I surrender to the swelling tide's unsearchable
depths. Enveloping, invading, saturating, and finally to indwell; I am
consumed by fullness of joy – still me, but me at peace. The stench of self
dissolves, washed away to depths unknown, and I become one with the
All.

Shekinah… the liquid glory washes over me pulsing with the pure
essence which flooded the heavens and brought forth the vast expanse of
galaxies we call home… yet not truly so yet. When that pulsing, swelling
tide reaches its fullness… consuming the farthest reaches of this mortal
plane… then, then we shall see glory reach its fullest expression –
swelling…consuming all throughout the untold, endless ages to come.

Michael M. Middleton

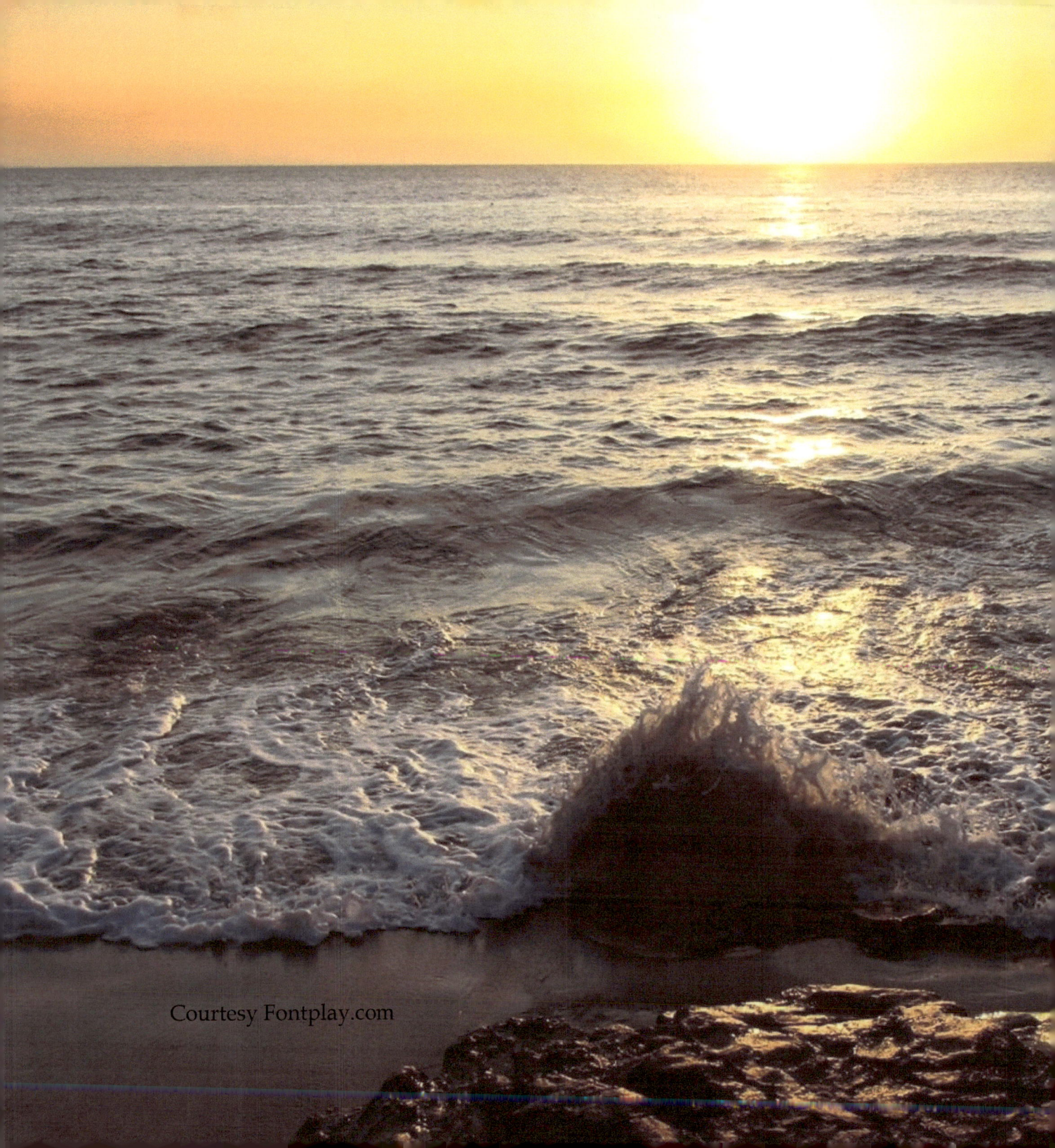

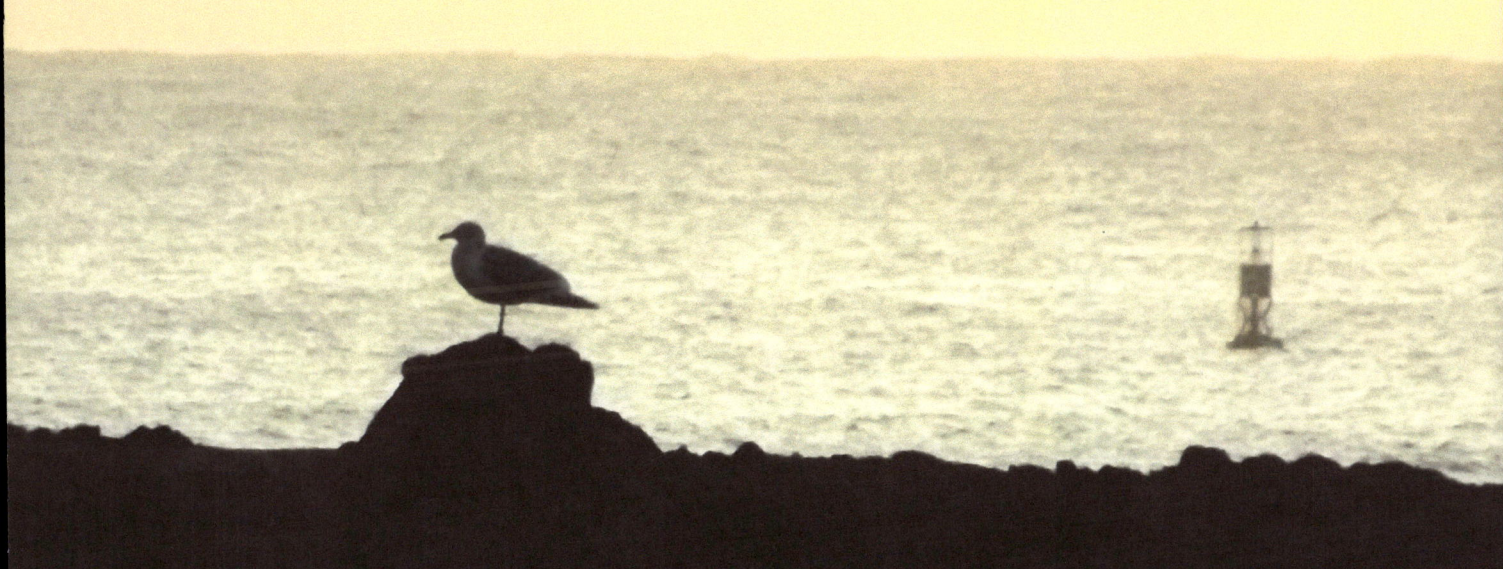

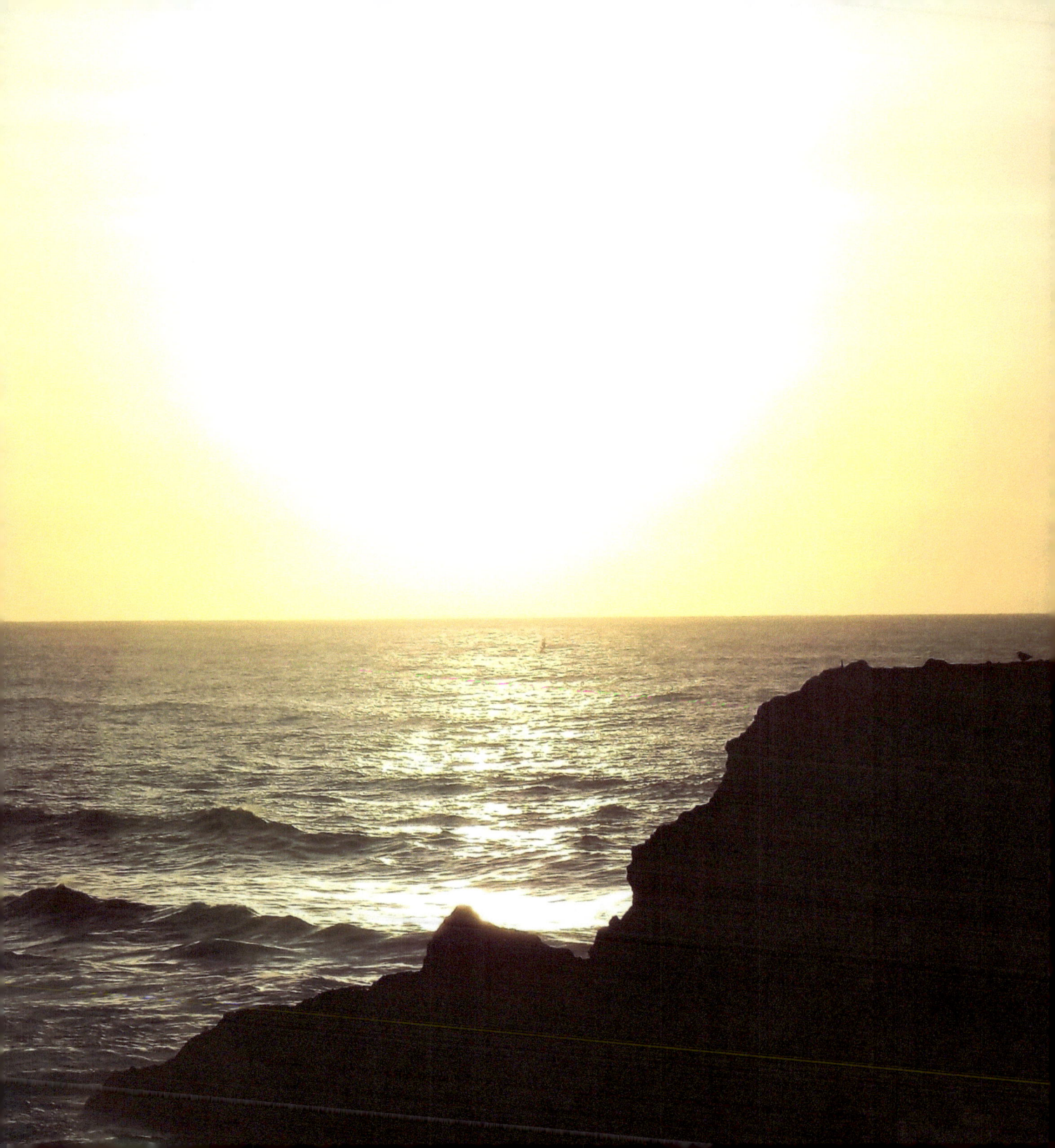

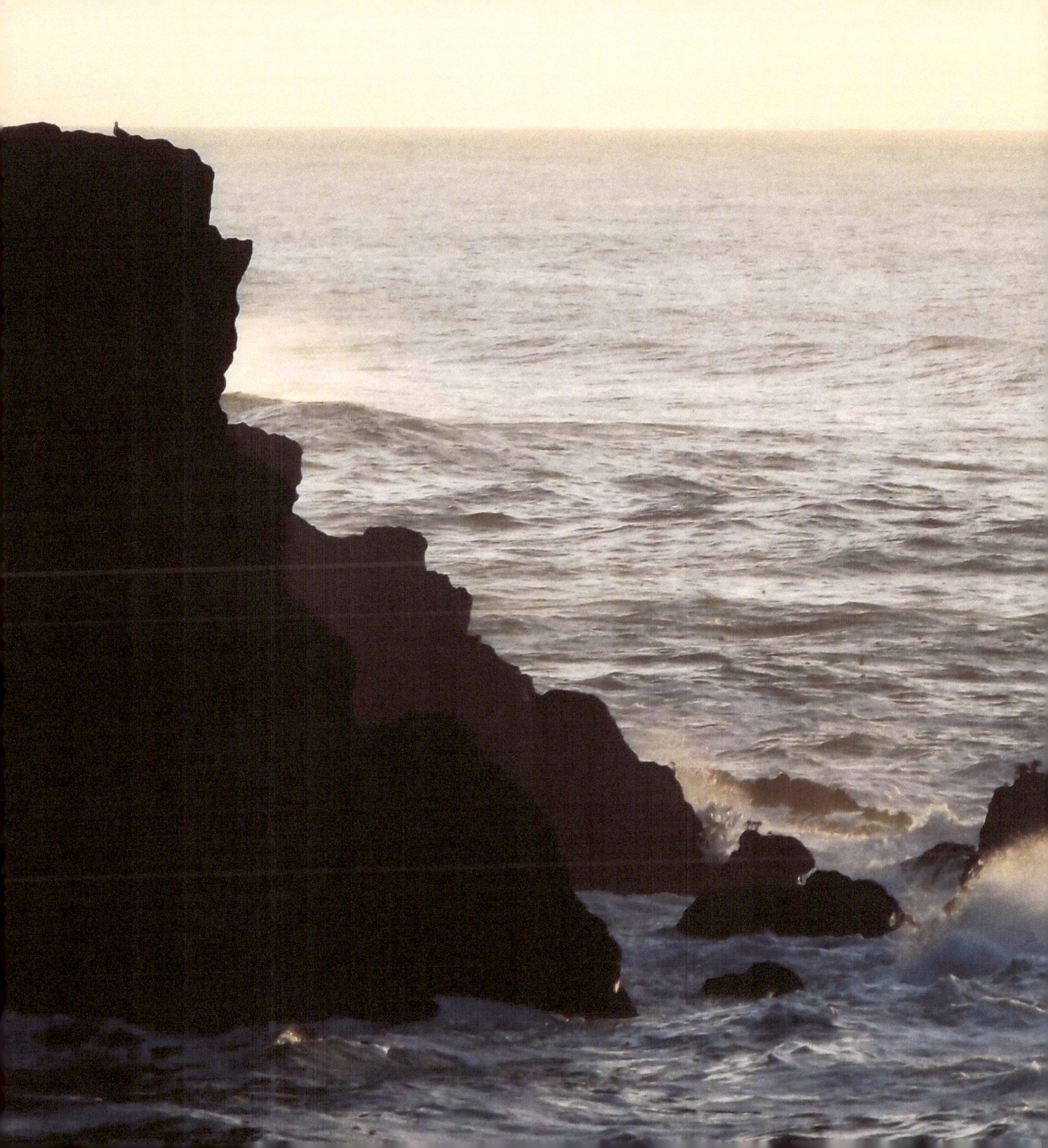

Beyond

Over the far horizon,
beyond the setting sun,
there lies a magic moment
when sea
and sky
are one.

Michael M. Middleton

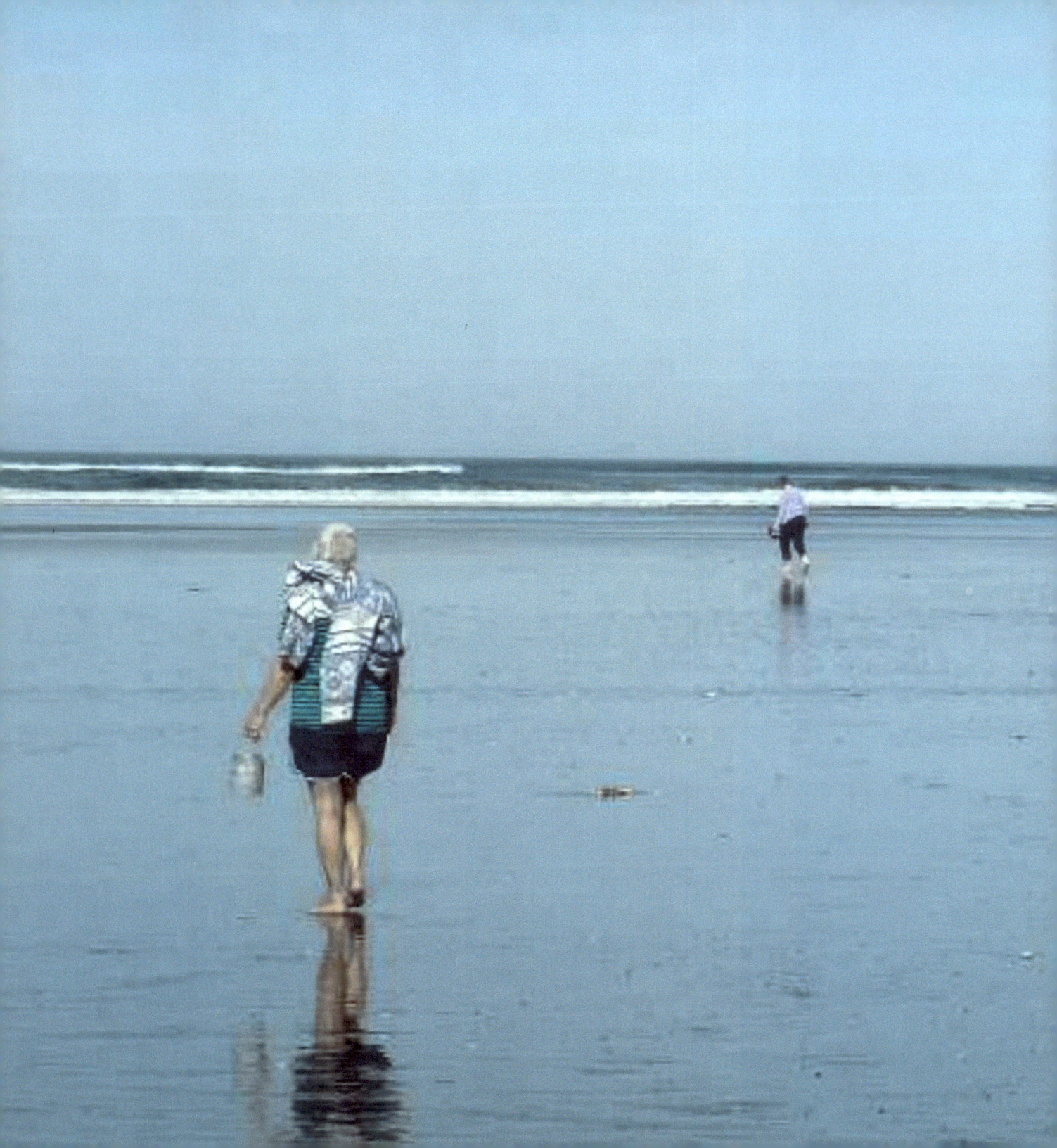

<u>Tidepool</u>

Mysterious islands of life
dapple the distant shore-
like solitary outposts of wonder,
until the lonely orb
swallows them once more.

Michael M. Middleton

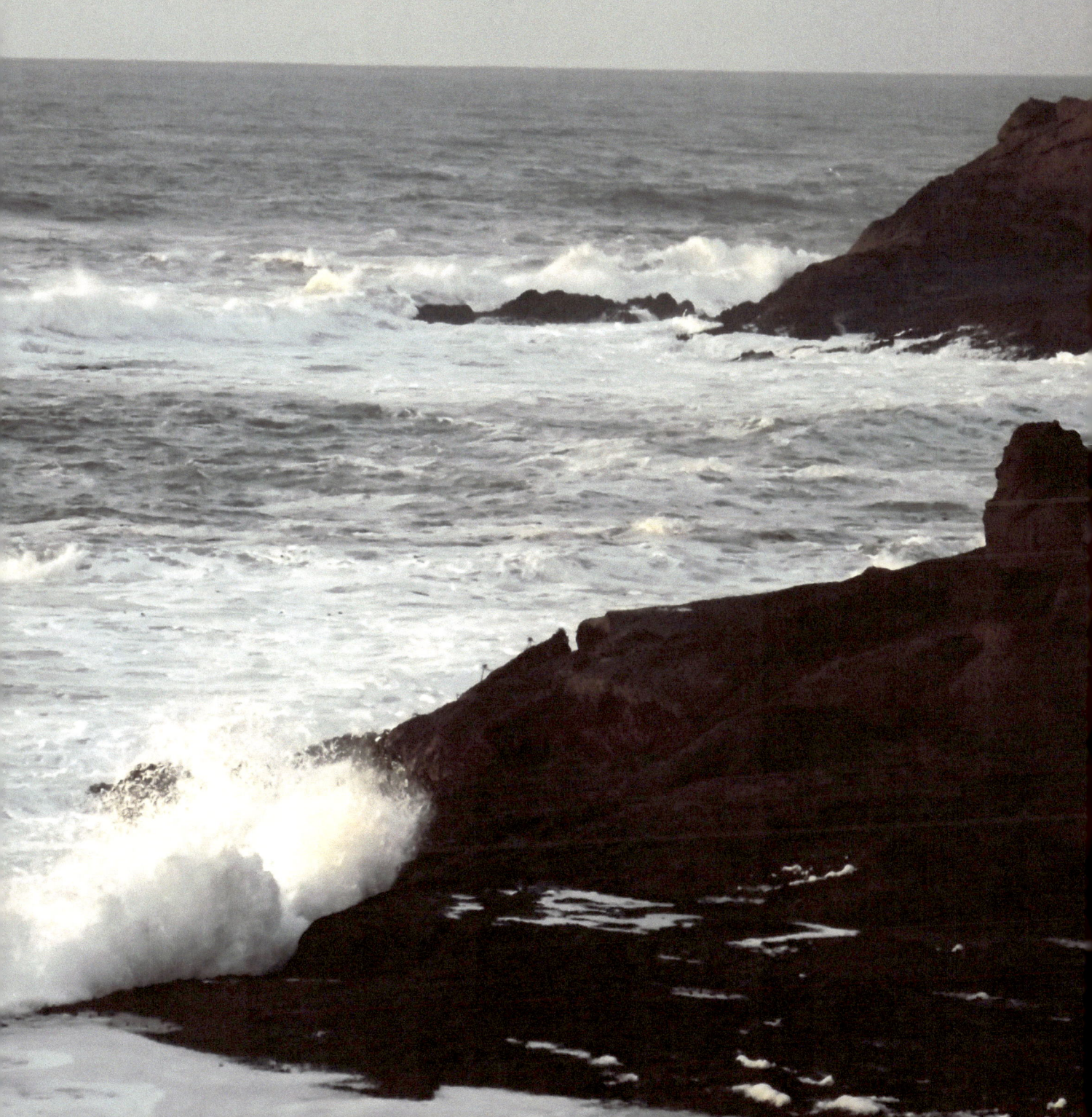

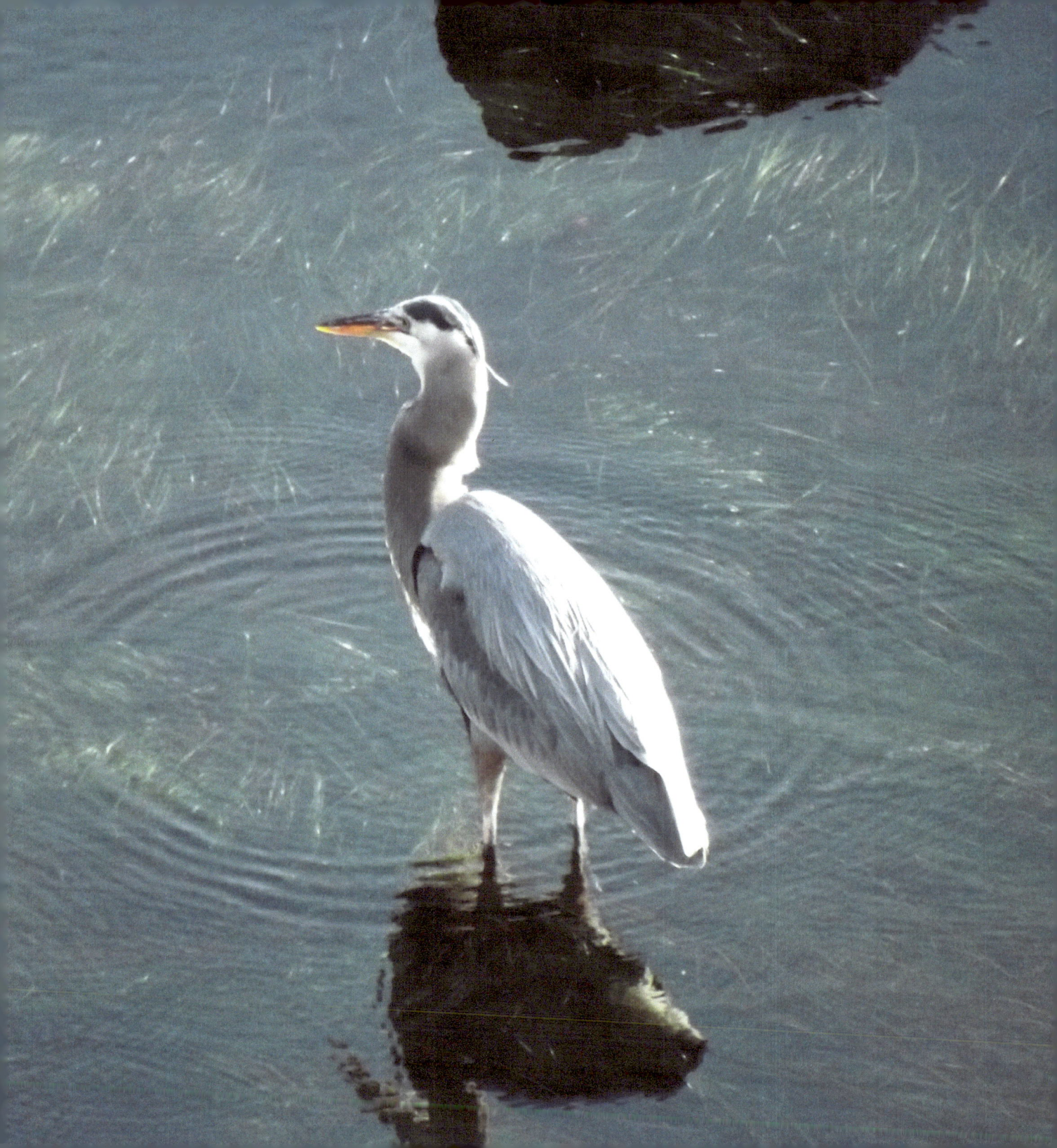

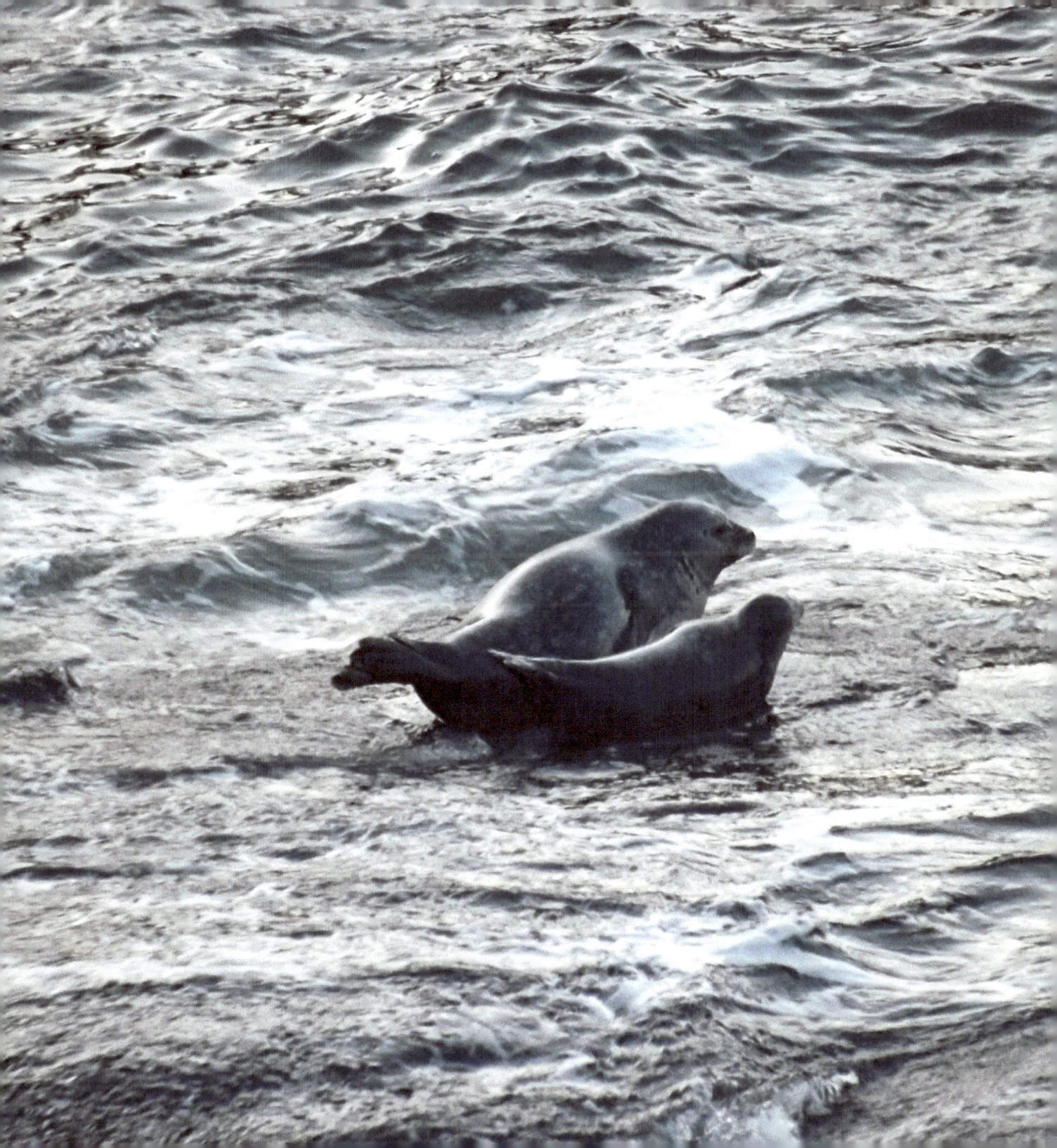

The River at Dawn

A ribbon of glass
slides slowly south, then west,
then south again it goes.
The day's first rays
in tangerine hue
enflame the festooned flow.
A wisp of white lace,
fleeing the heat,
drapes upon the glass.
The day fully breaks;
the lace melts away-
all meager things must pass.

Michael M. Middleton

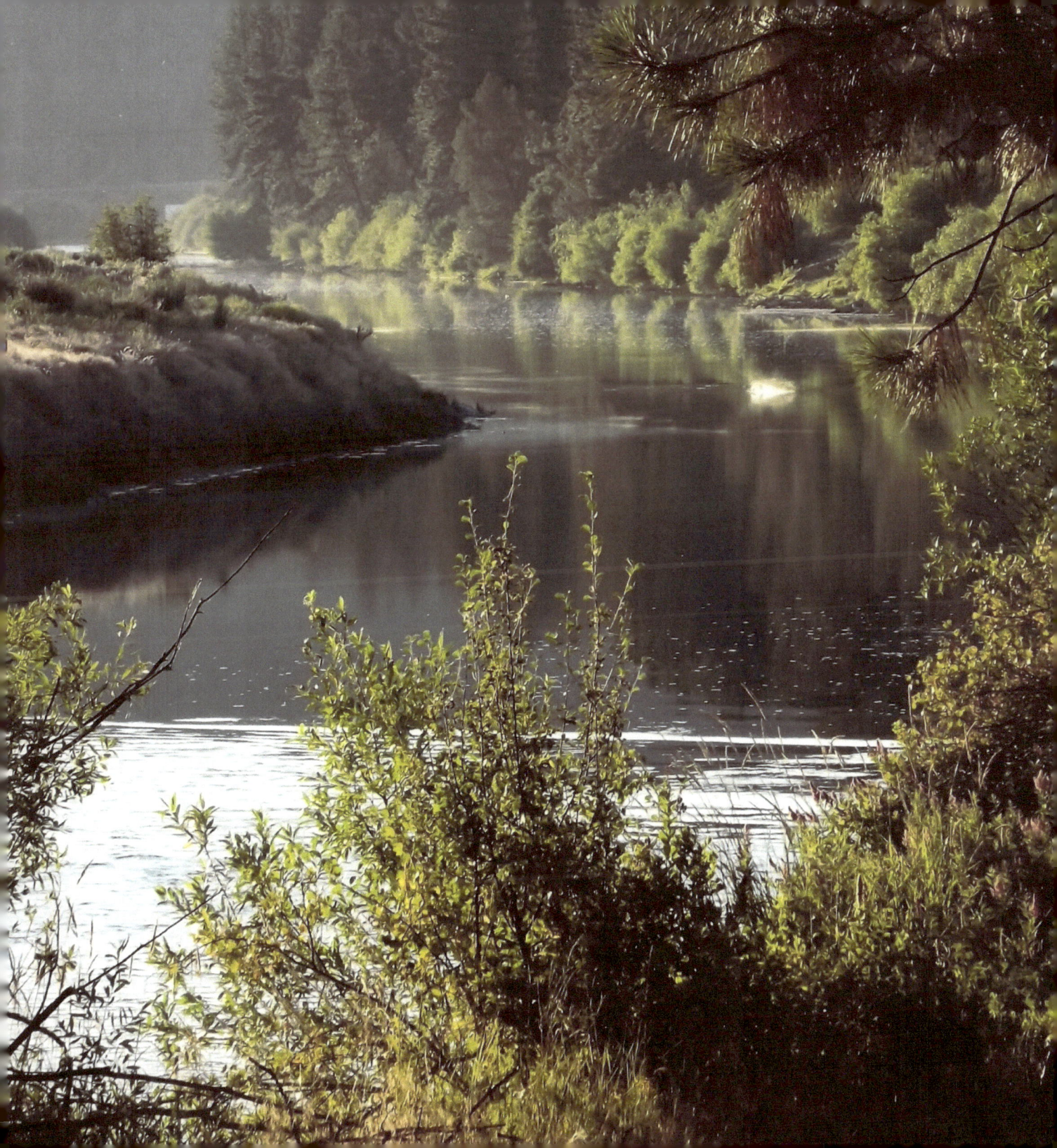

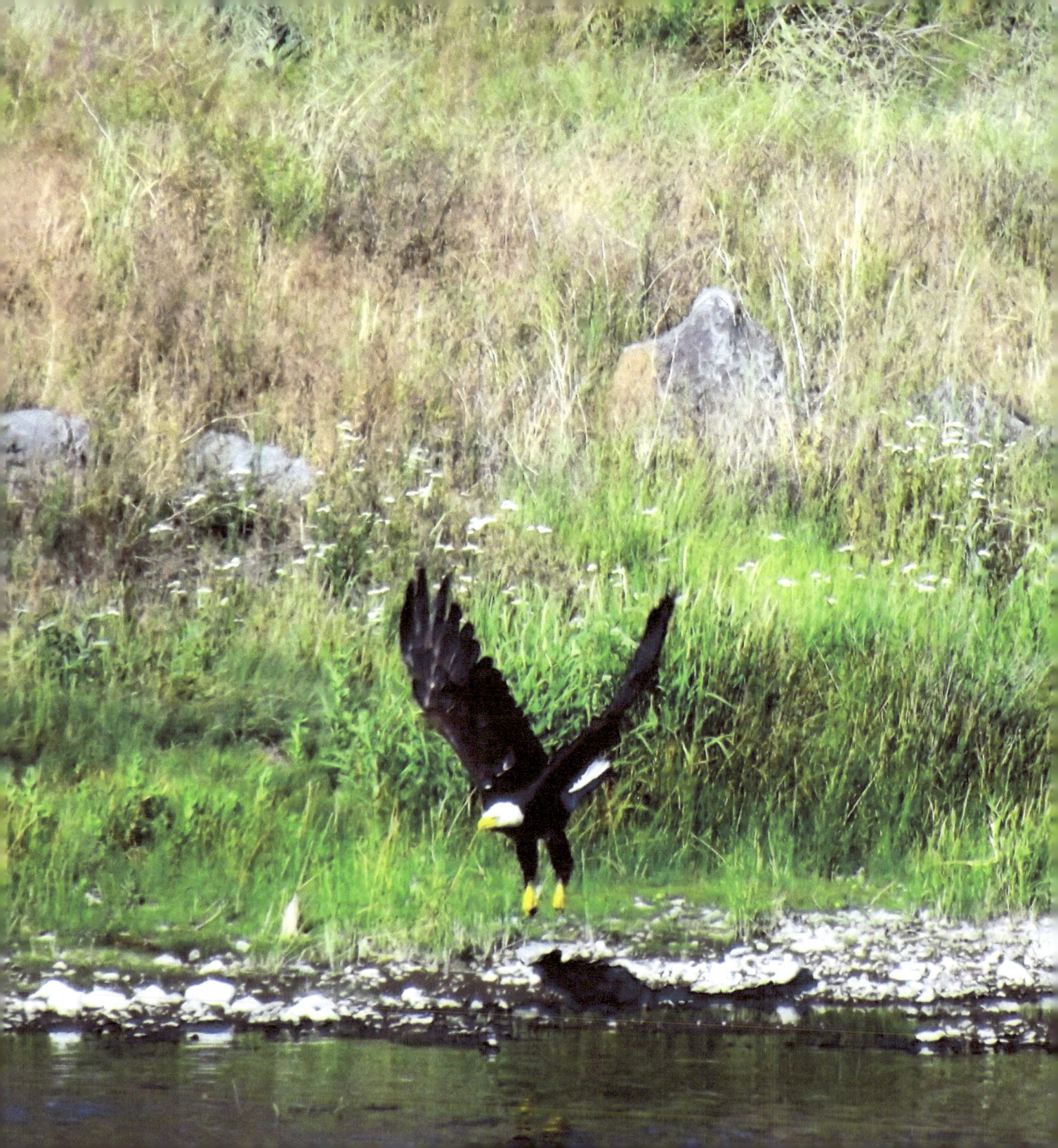

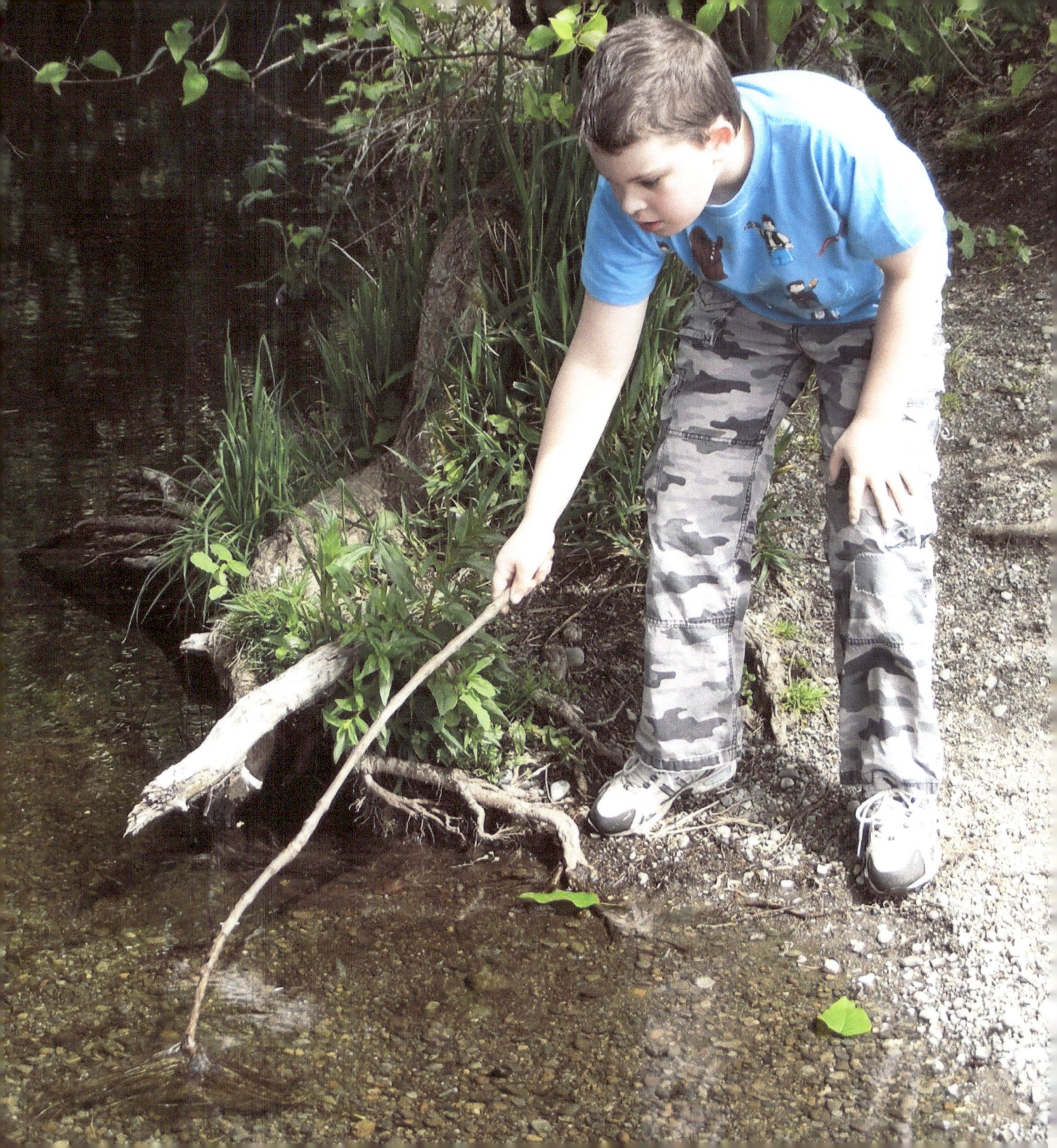

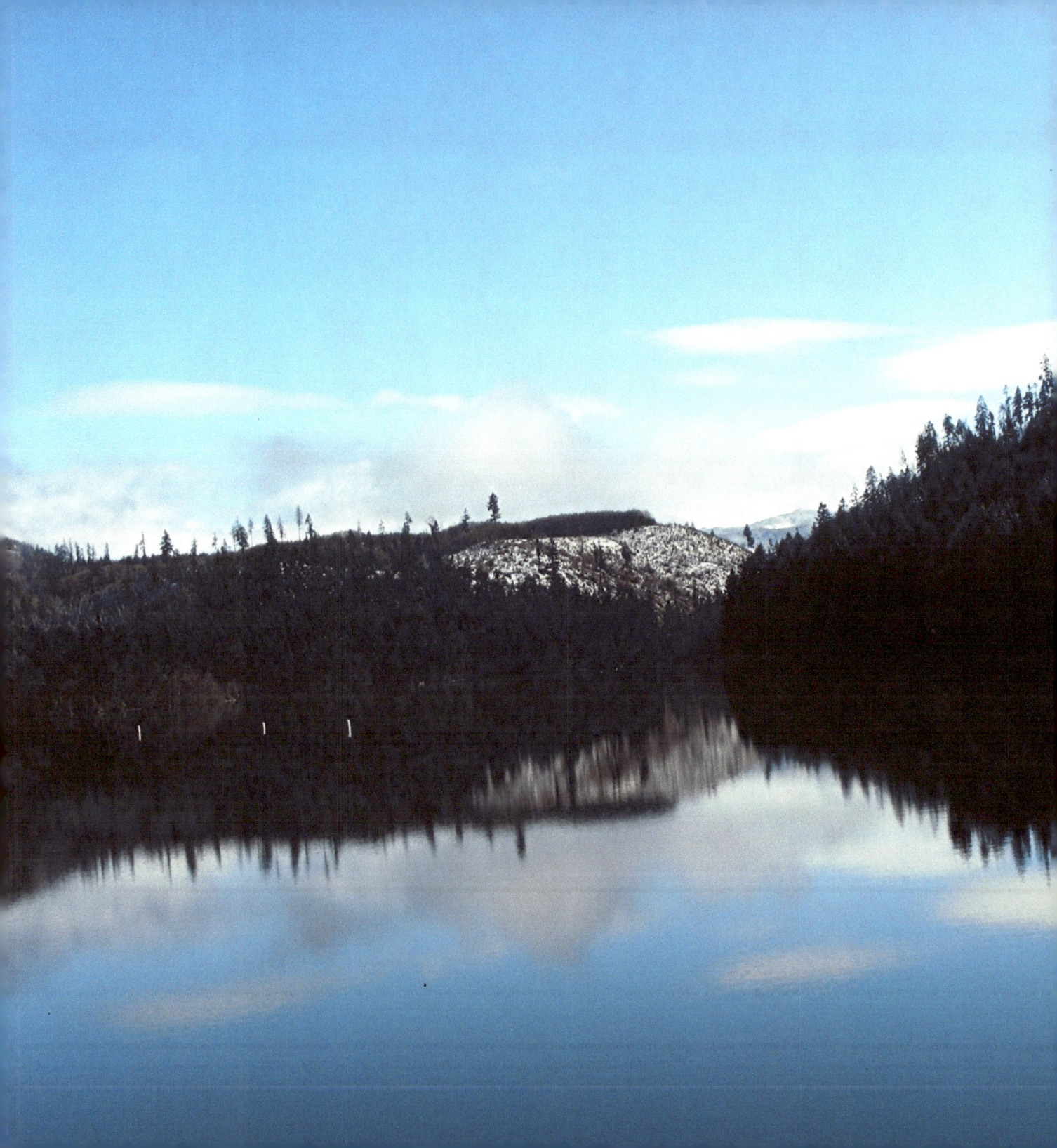

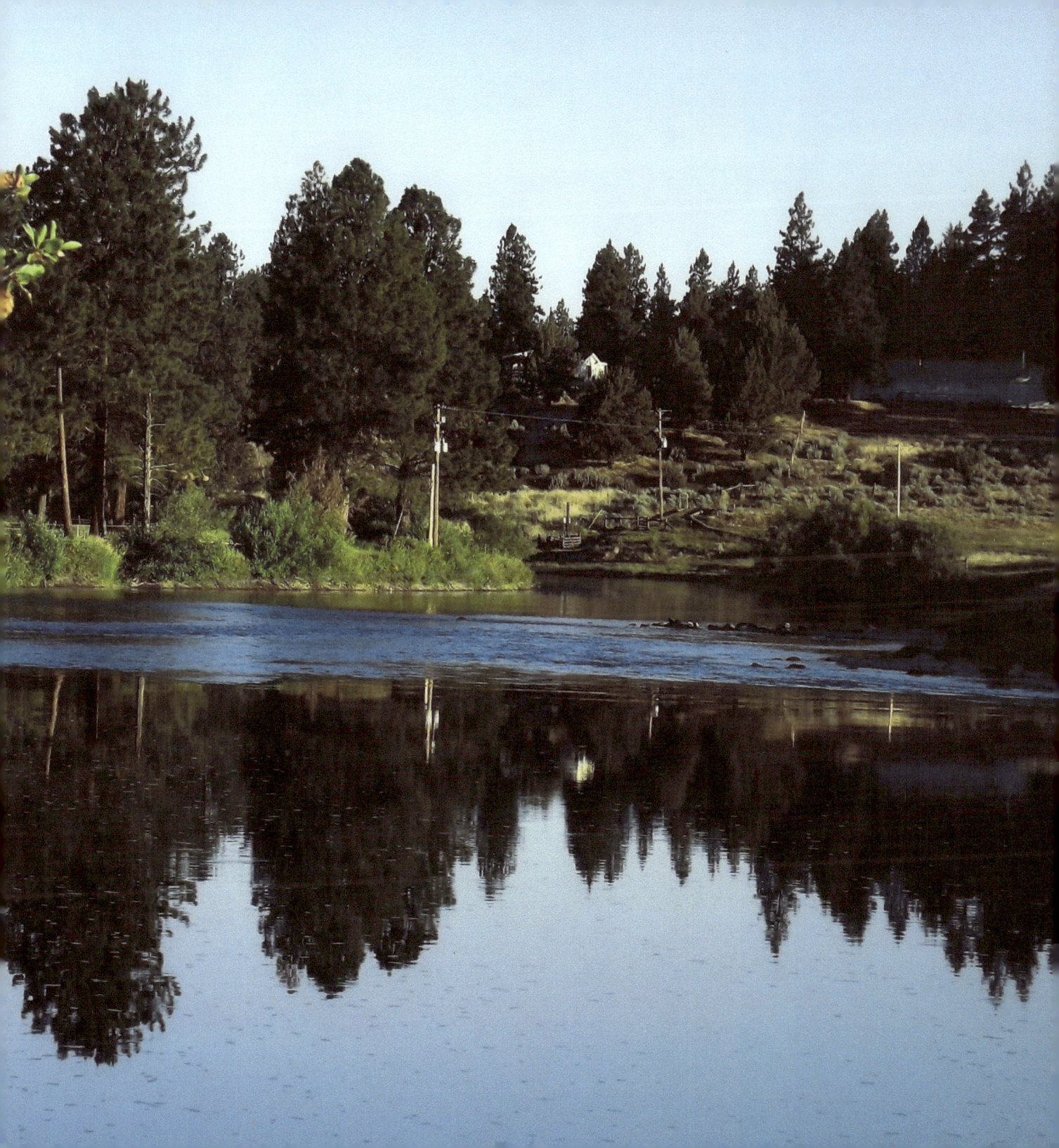

Pacific

An endless expanse of sullen sky
blankets the gray-green sea;
tumbling brine grinds stone to sand
and drags it to the deep.
A frigid mist,
partly sky and partly surf
stabs the flesh
as it drapes to quench the earth.

Distant calls
of gull
and coot
and crow
strangely mesh
with unheard, unsung songs
somewhere deep within my soul.

The wind,
the waves,
the surging rhythm
of this place
strangely speaks
of power,
of peace,
of perfect wisdom
and unyielding grace.

Michael M. Middleton

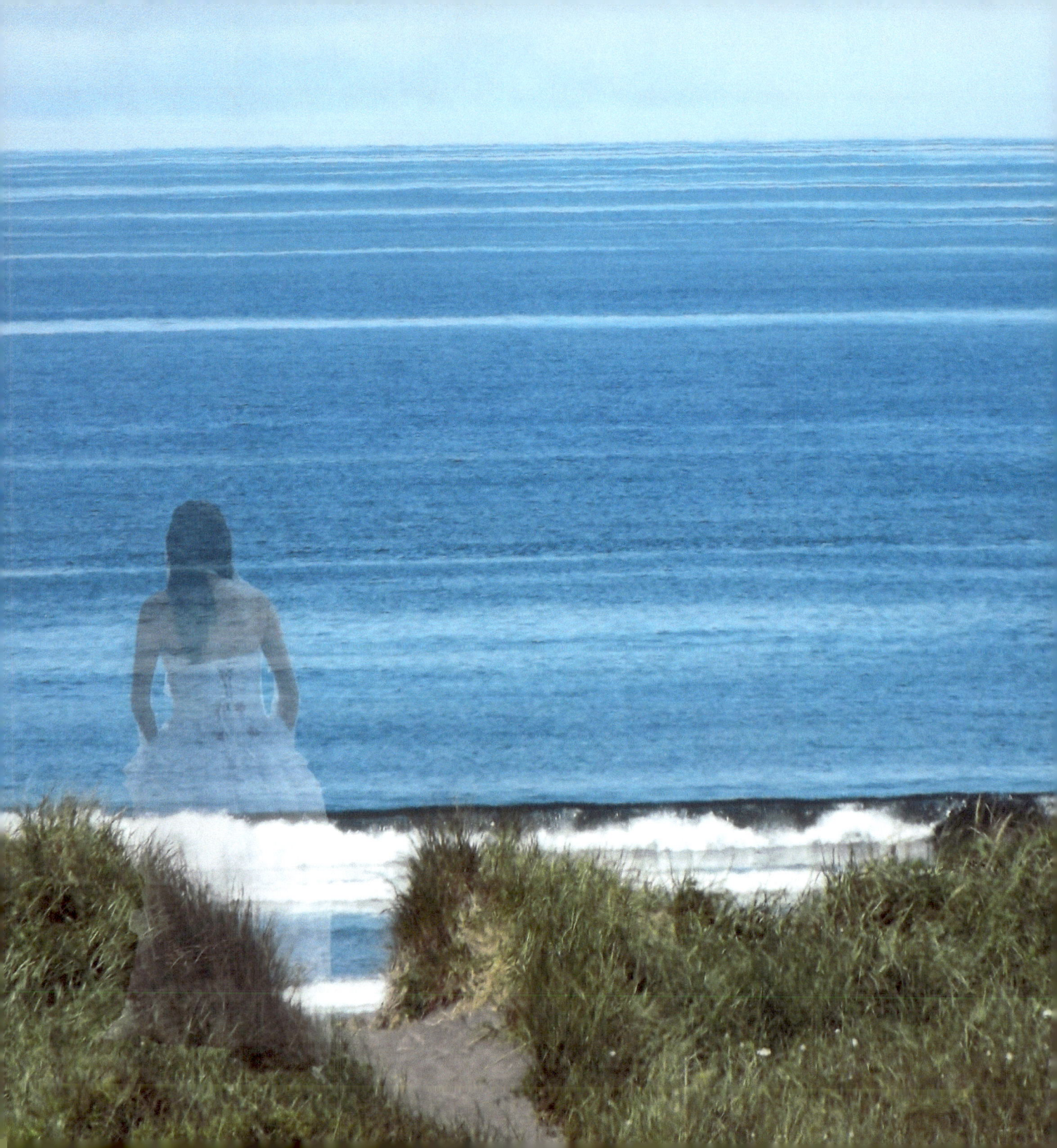

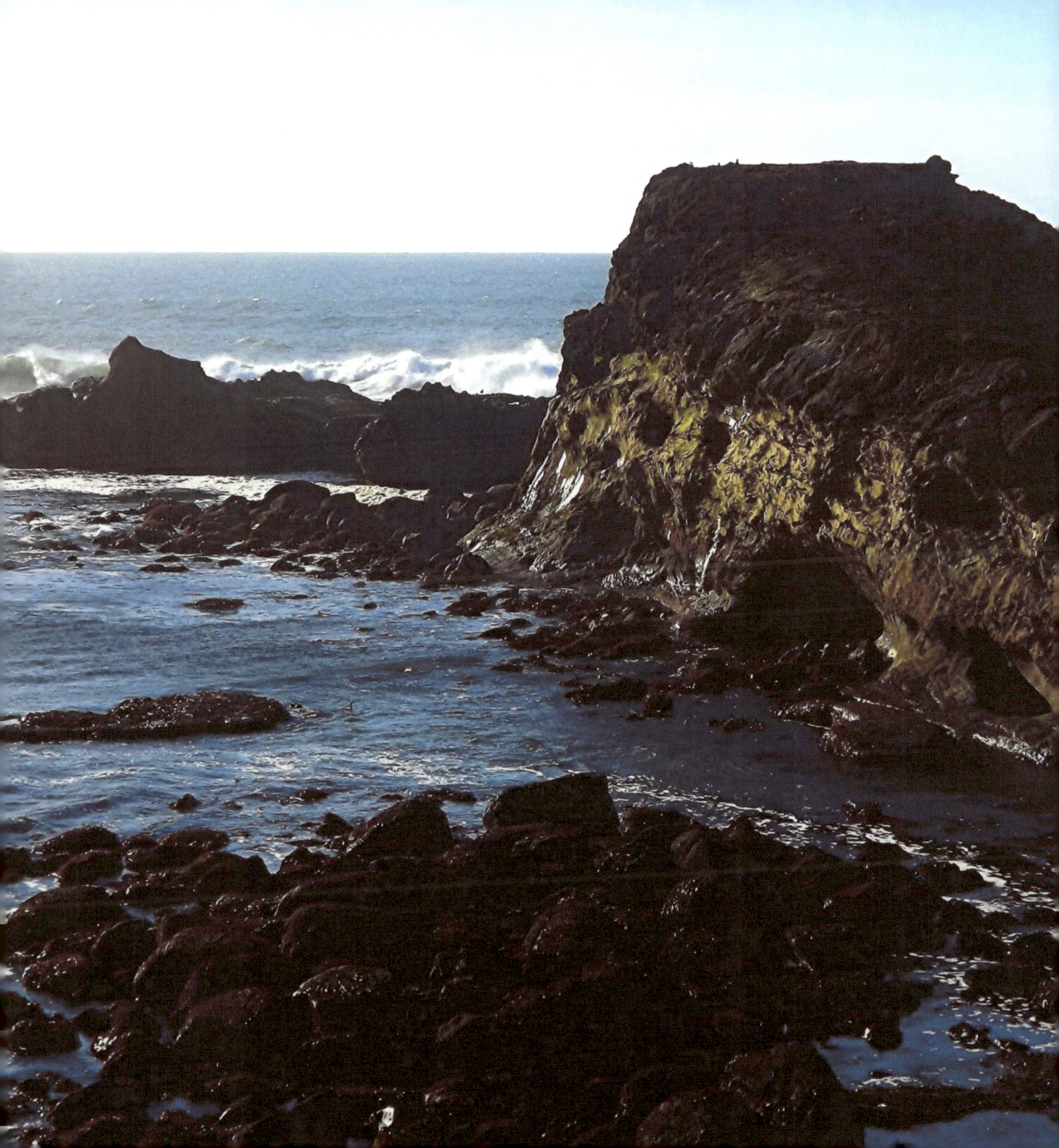

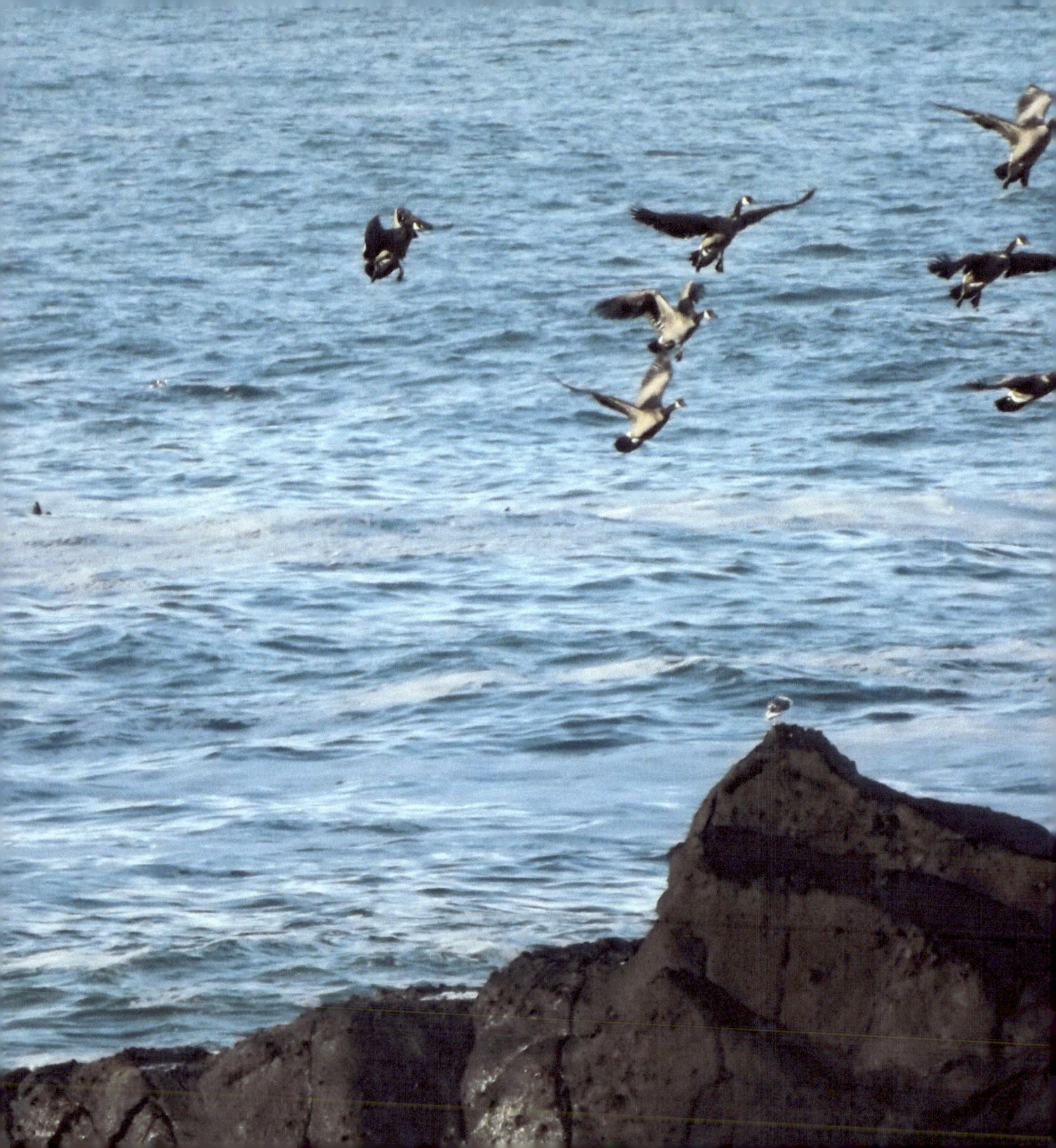

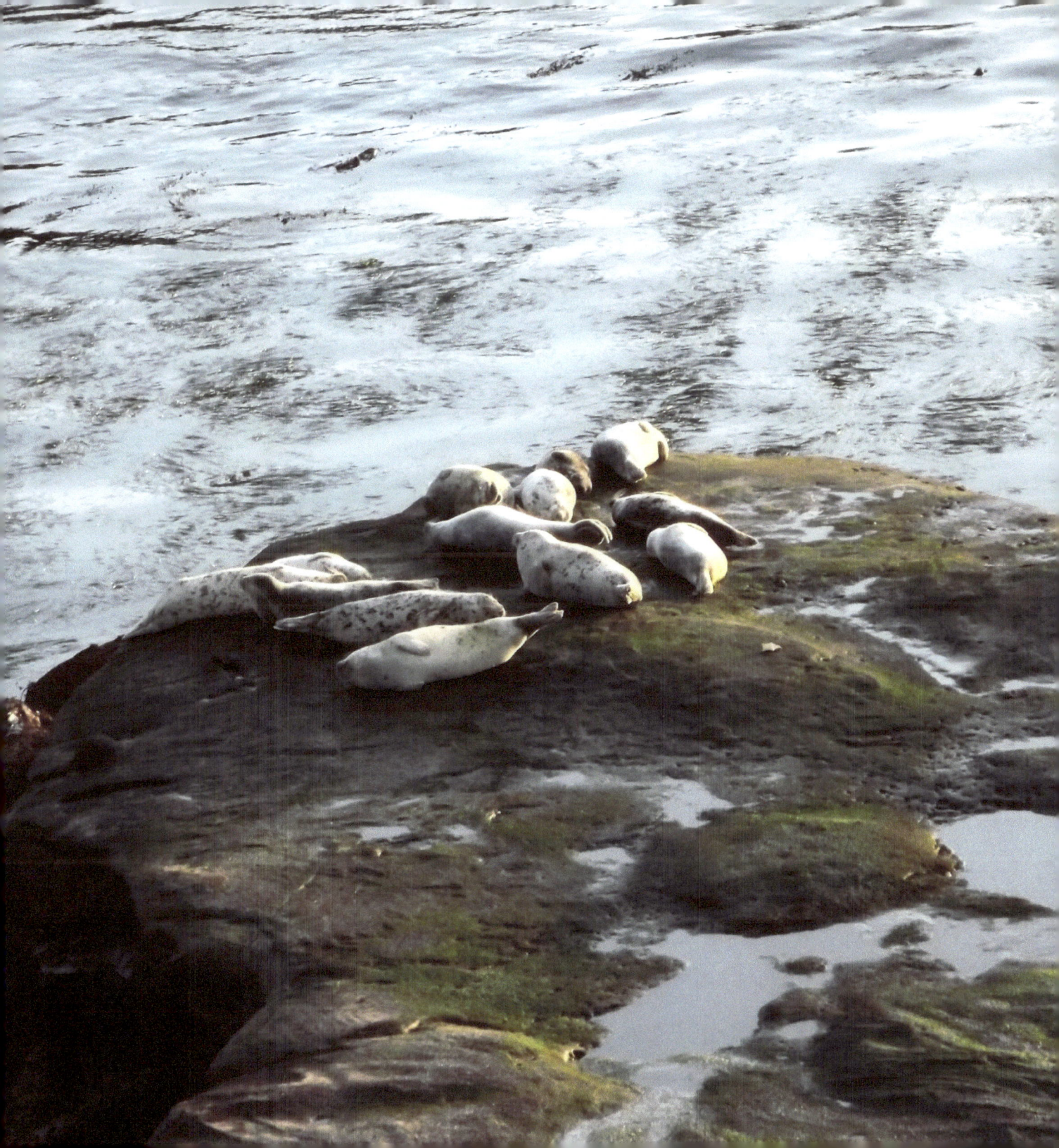

The Lighthouse

Perched atop a lonely spire,
thrown against the sea,
beckoning those who roam;
silent fire,
precise and measured,
calls the wayward home.

Michael M. Middleton

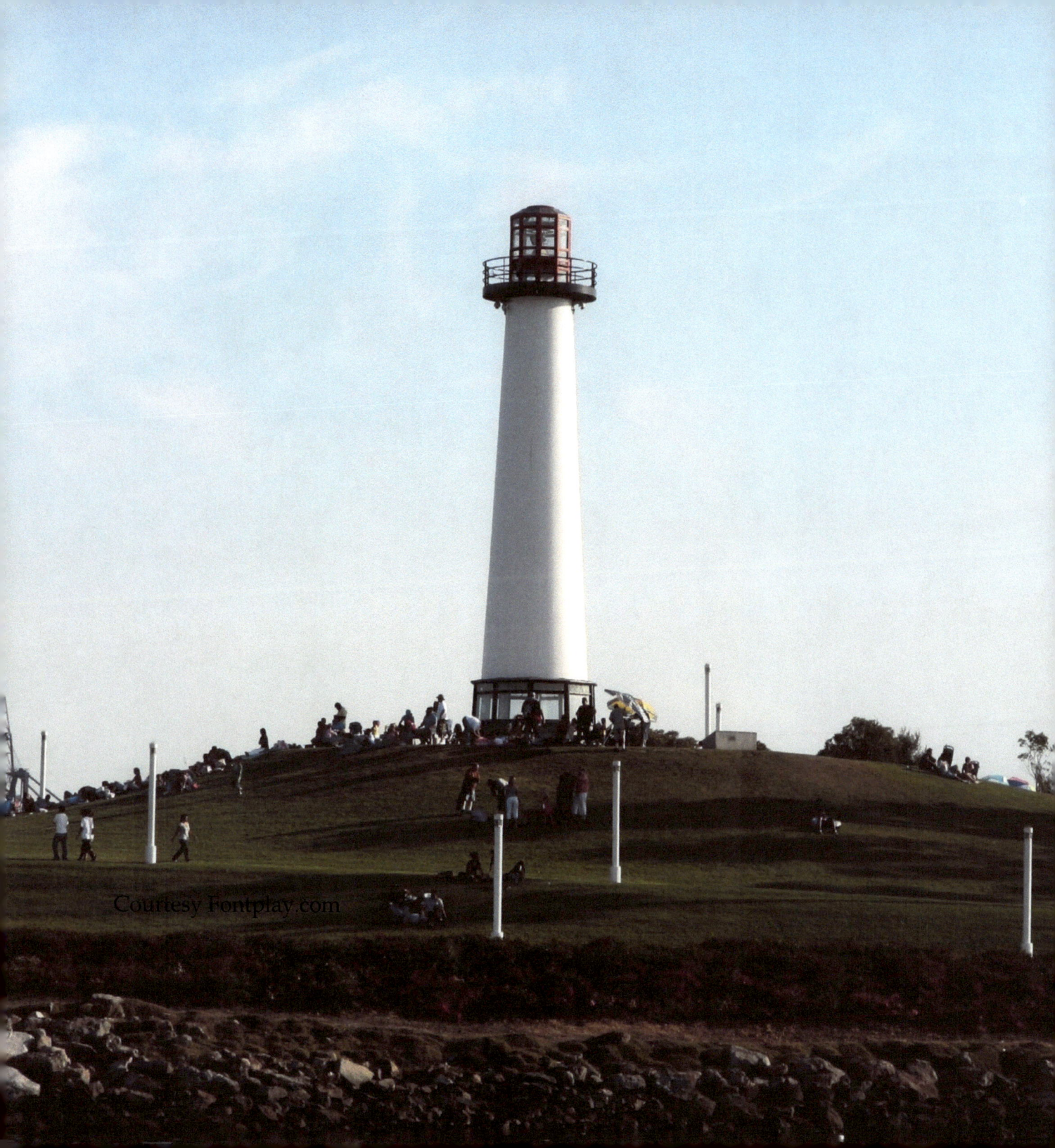

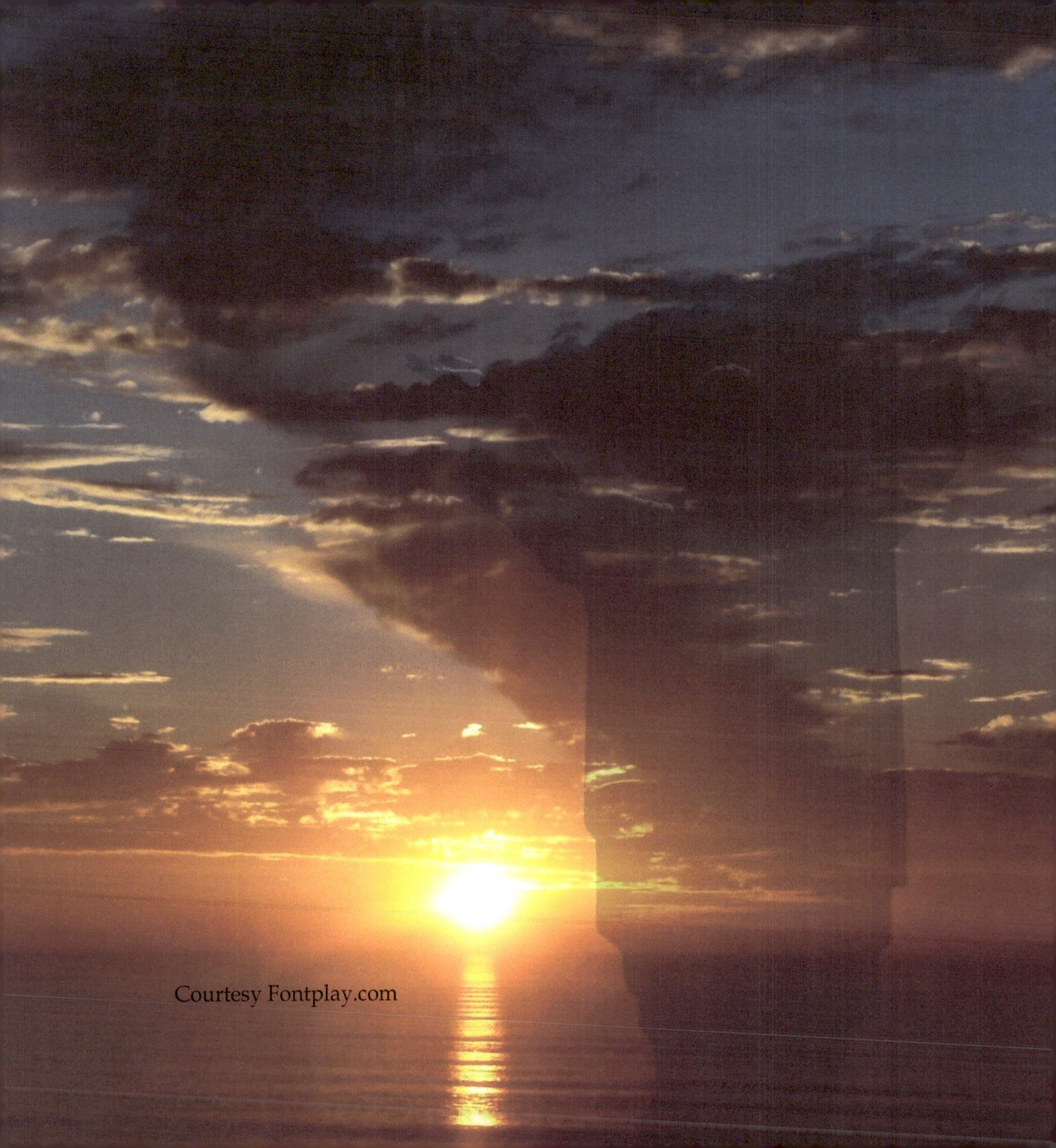

Courtesy Fontplay.com

Dancing With the Sea

If you would touch God
then wade out into the deep
and dance with the sea.

The deep's embrace
lays hold of grace
and sets the spirit free.

Michael M. Middleton

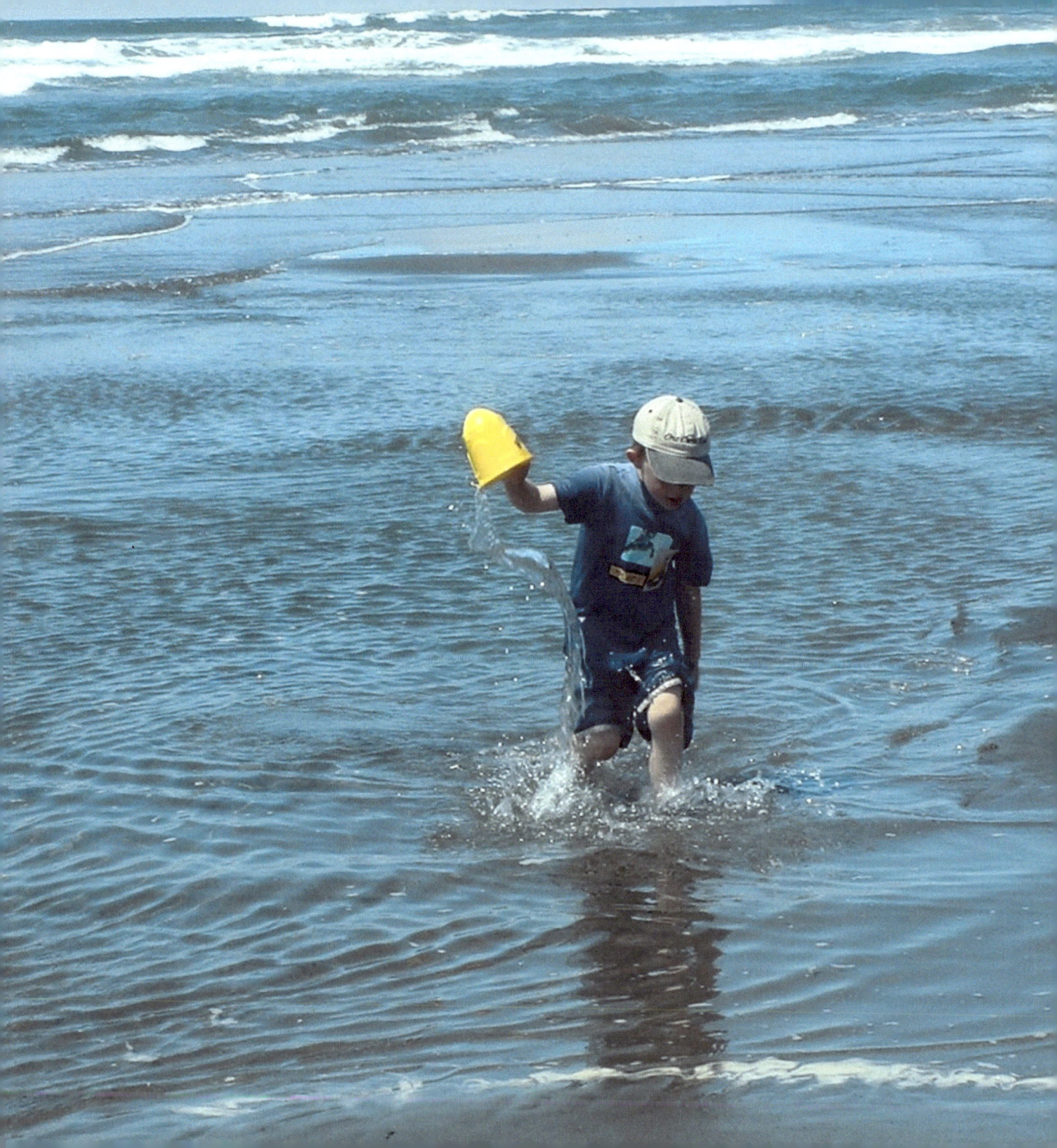

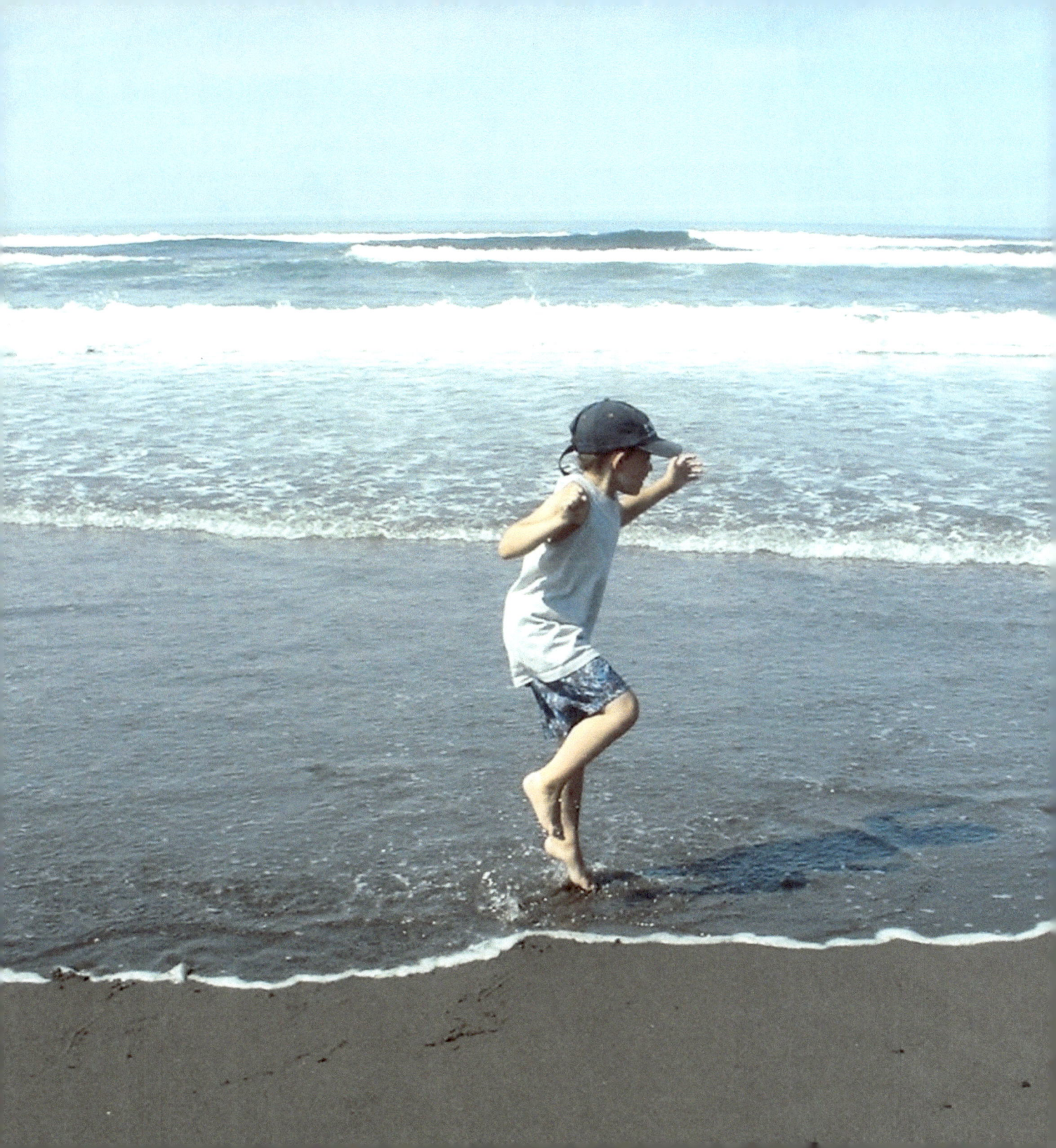

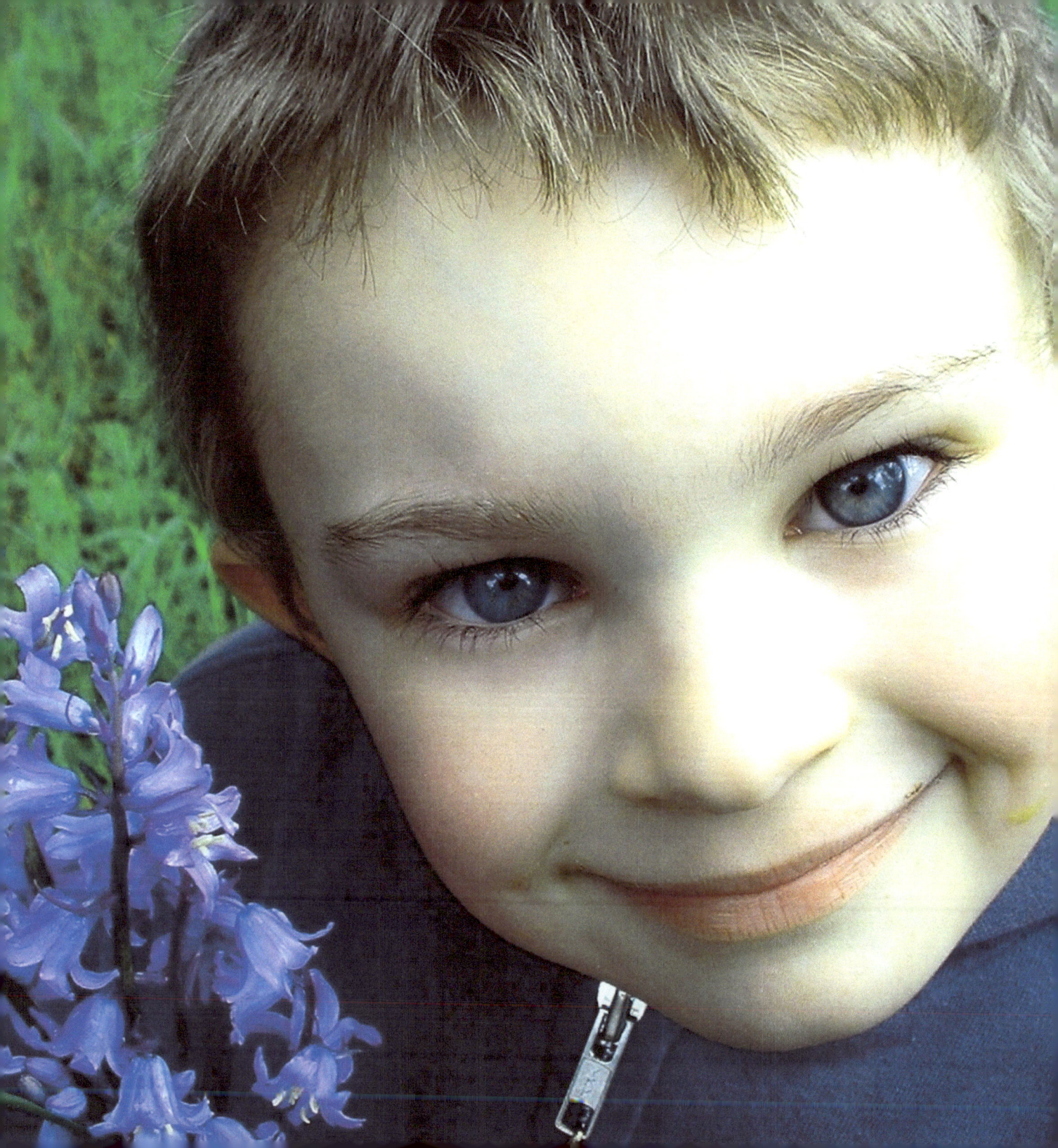

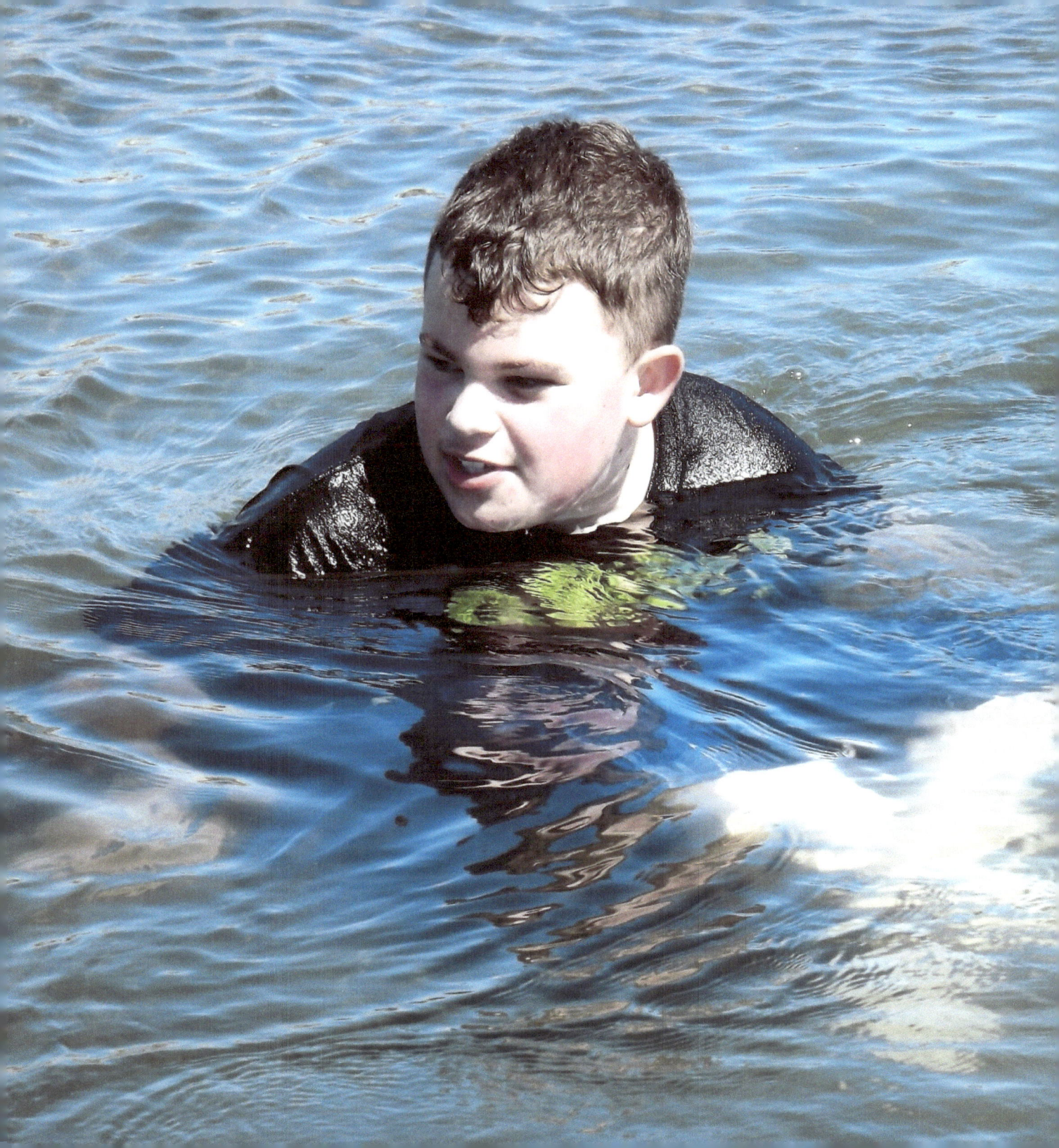

The Waterfall

The sleepy stream suddenly stirs,
awakened by gravity and stone.
As crystal waters fall and shatter,
silent voices suddenly sing
in soft and soothing tones.
As the flow quickens its march
it lunges and surges and soars.
The melody swells,
the song grows bolder;
the whisper becomes a roar.
Frantically leaping over the ledge,
the icy torrent fractures and frays.
Sheared by the wind
and freed by the fall,
it dissolves into silver spray.
Michael M. Middleton

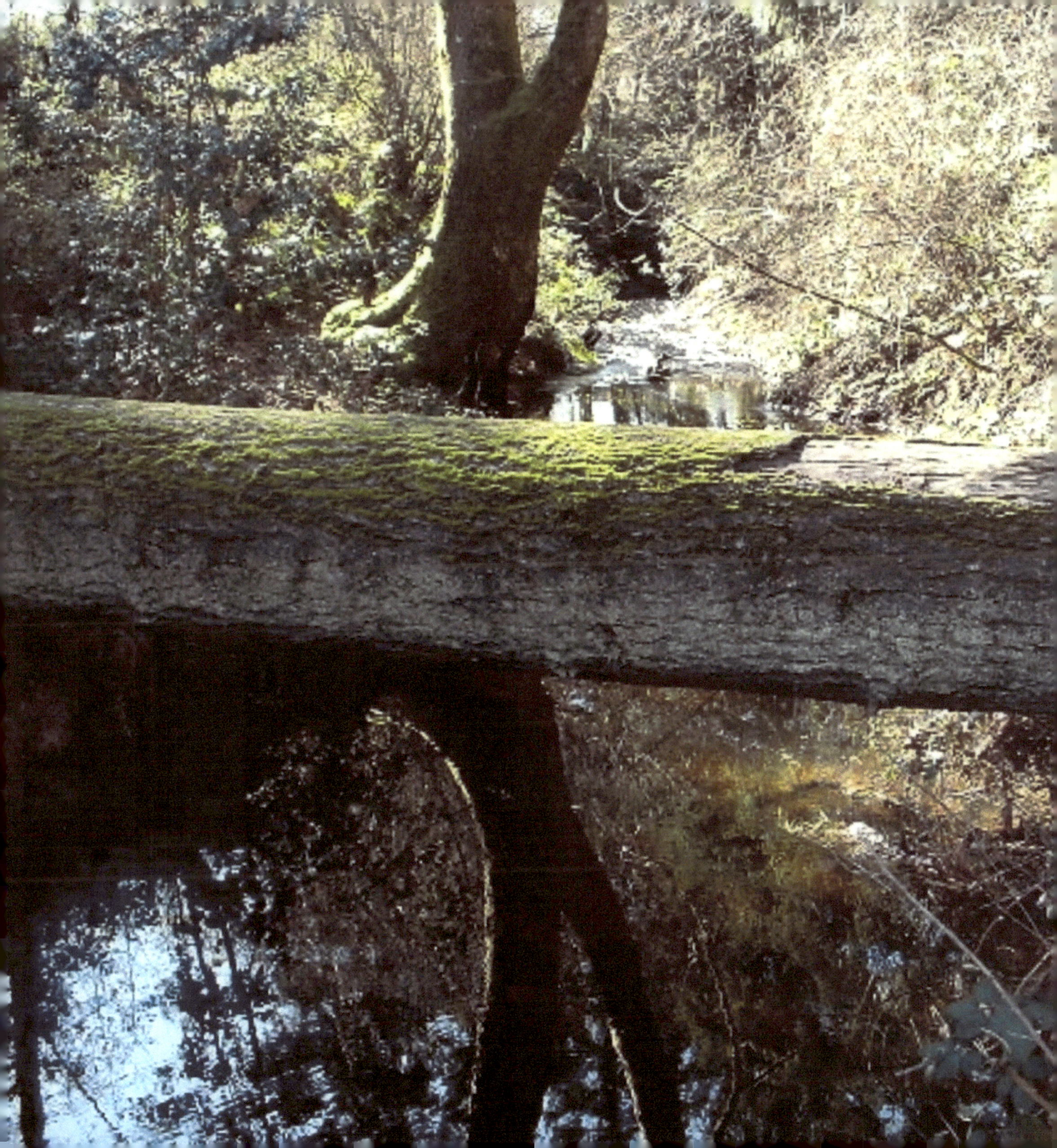

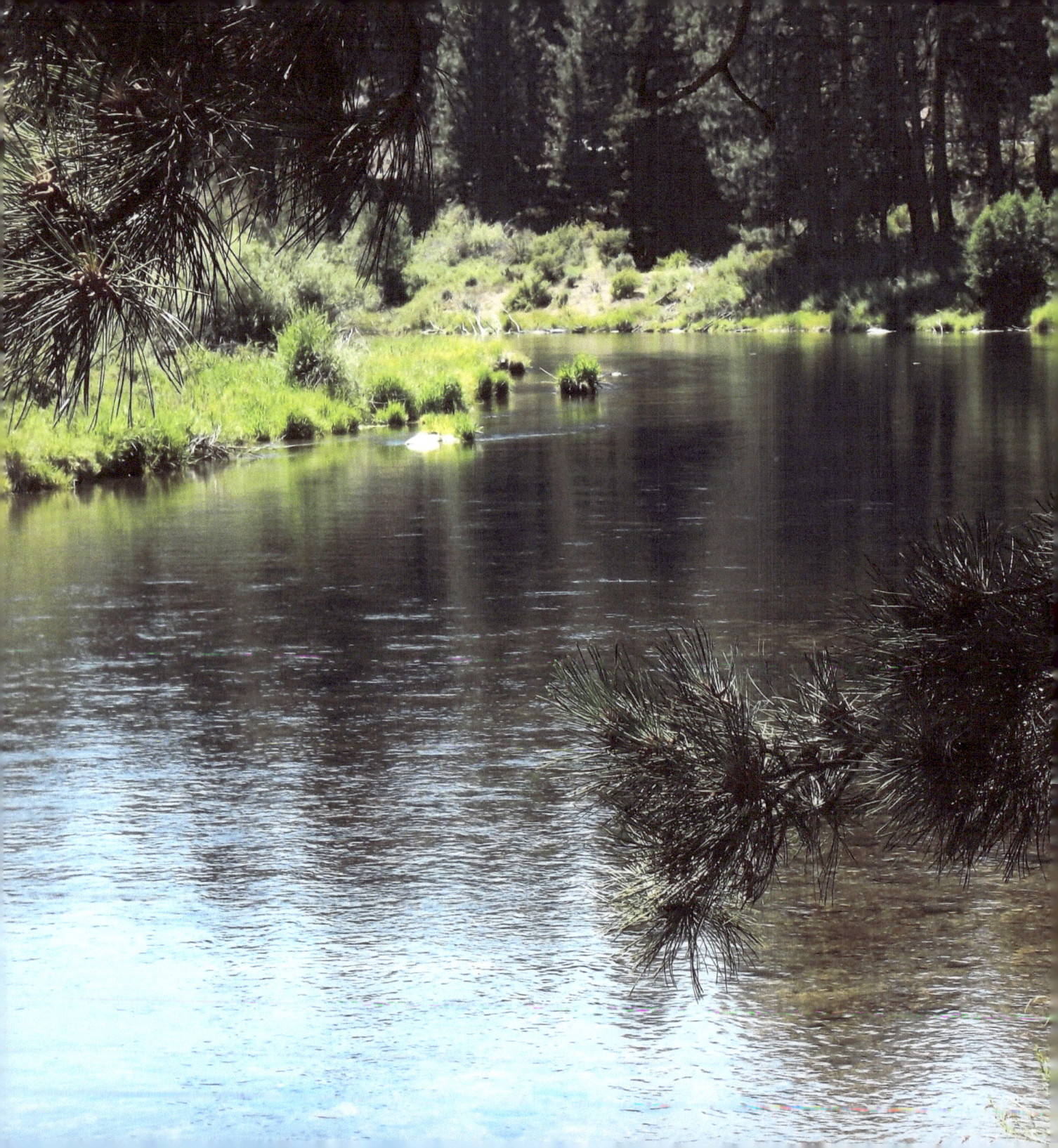

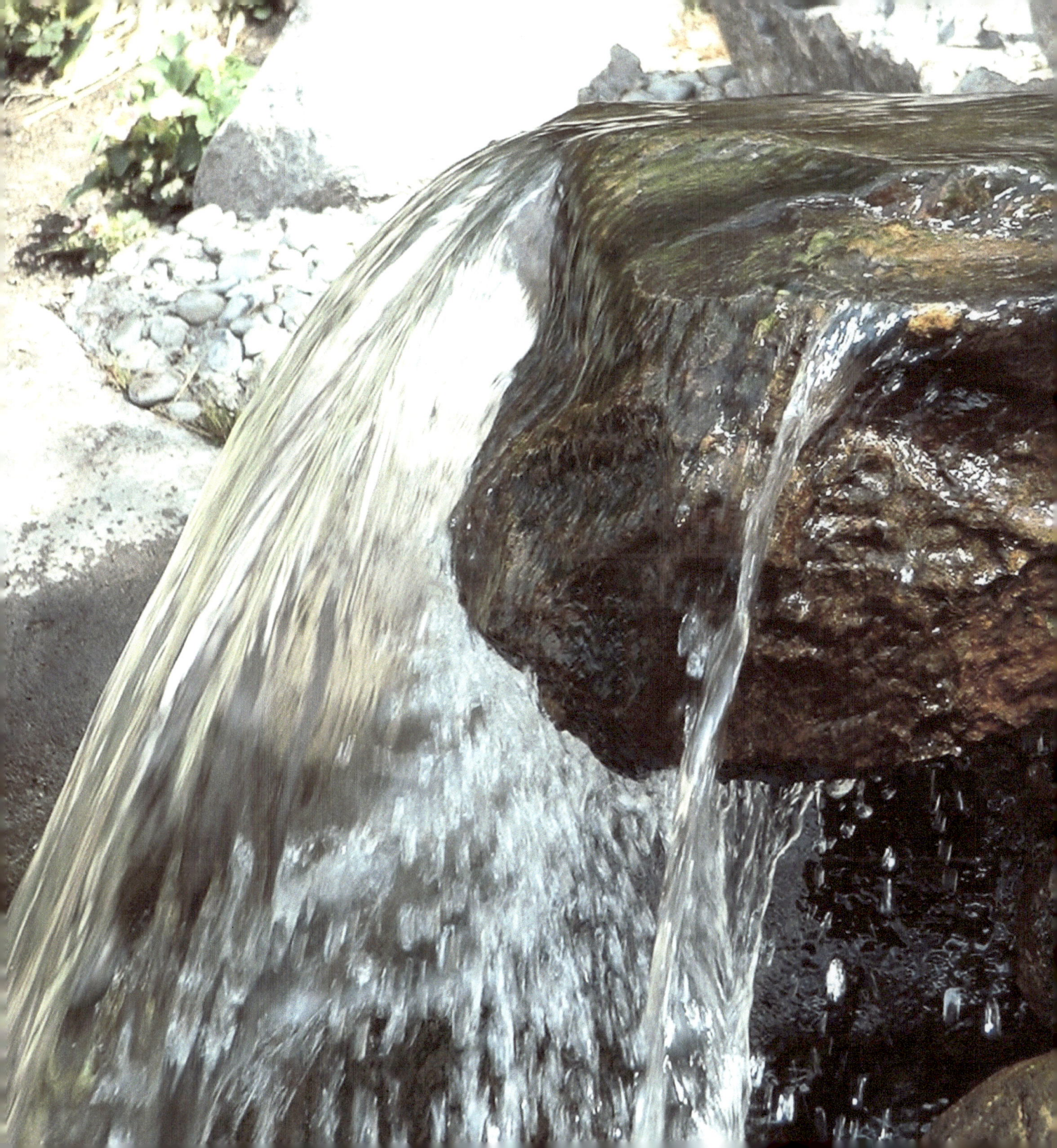

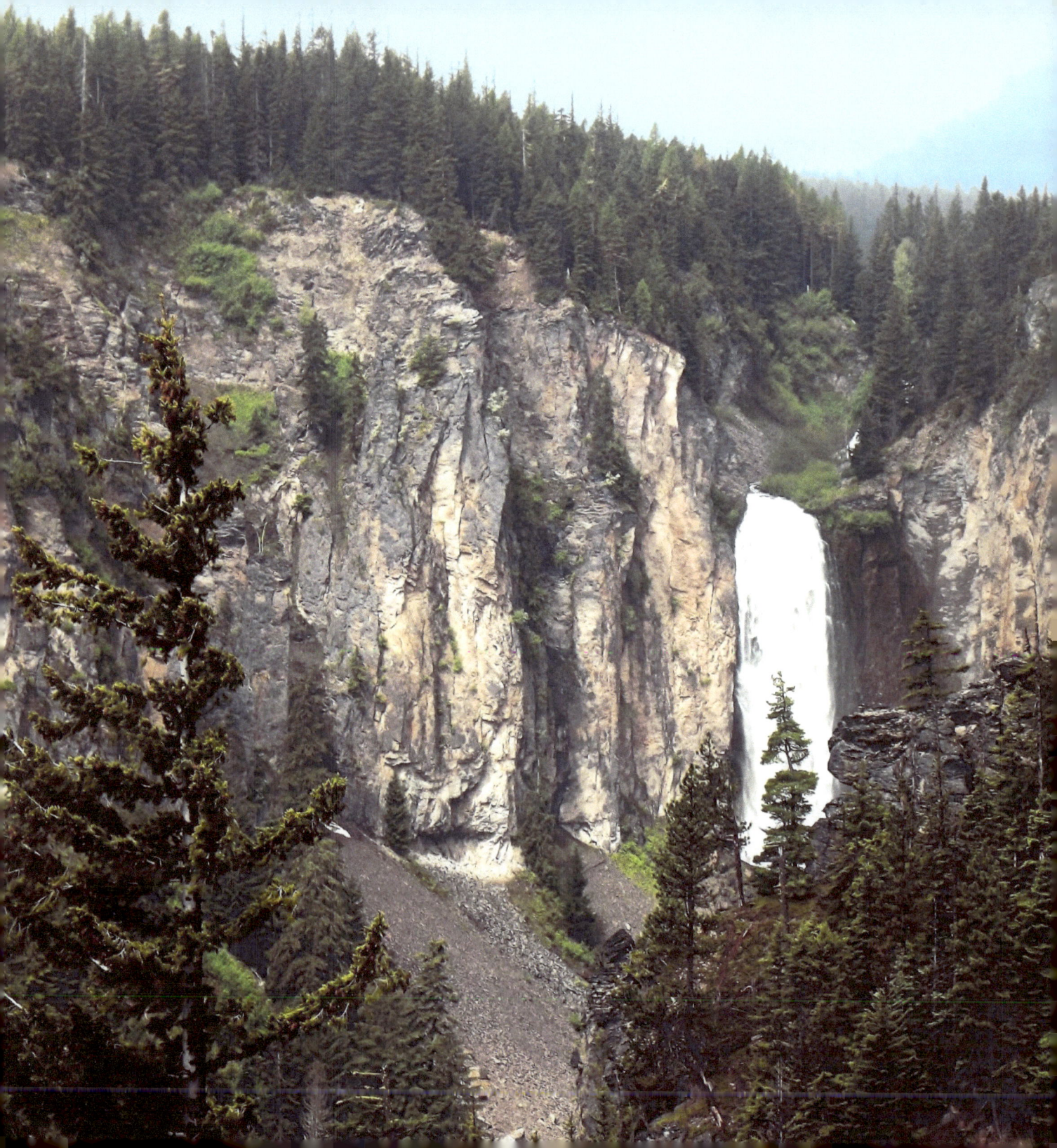

Counting Sand

I try to probe the mind of God;
to see all the whys and comprehend the how
and catch a glimpse of when.
My mind of flesh, a prisoner of time,
reaches with all of its reason
to see beyond what came before…
I stretch with all of my being
to grasp the eons past, beyond the beginning,
when the all-in-all was all there was…
trying to understand
what 'limitless' really means.
To be without end I may just comprehend,
but how can one be…without beginning?
Questions unanswered, I guess they'll never be;
I might just as well sit on the beach
counting sand.

Michael M. Middleton

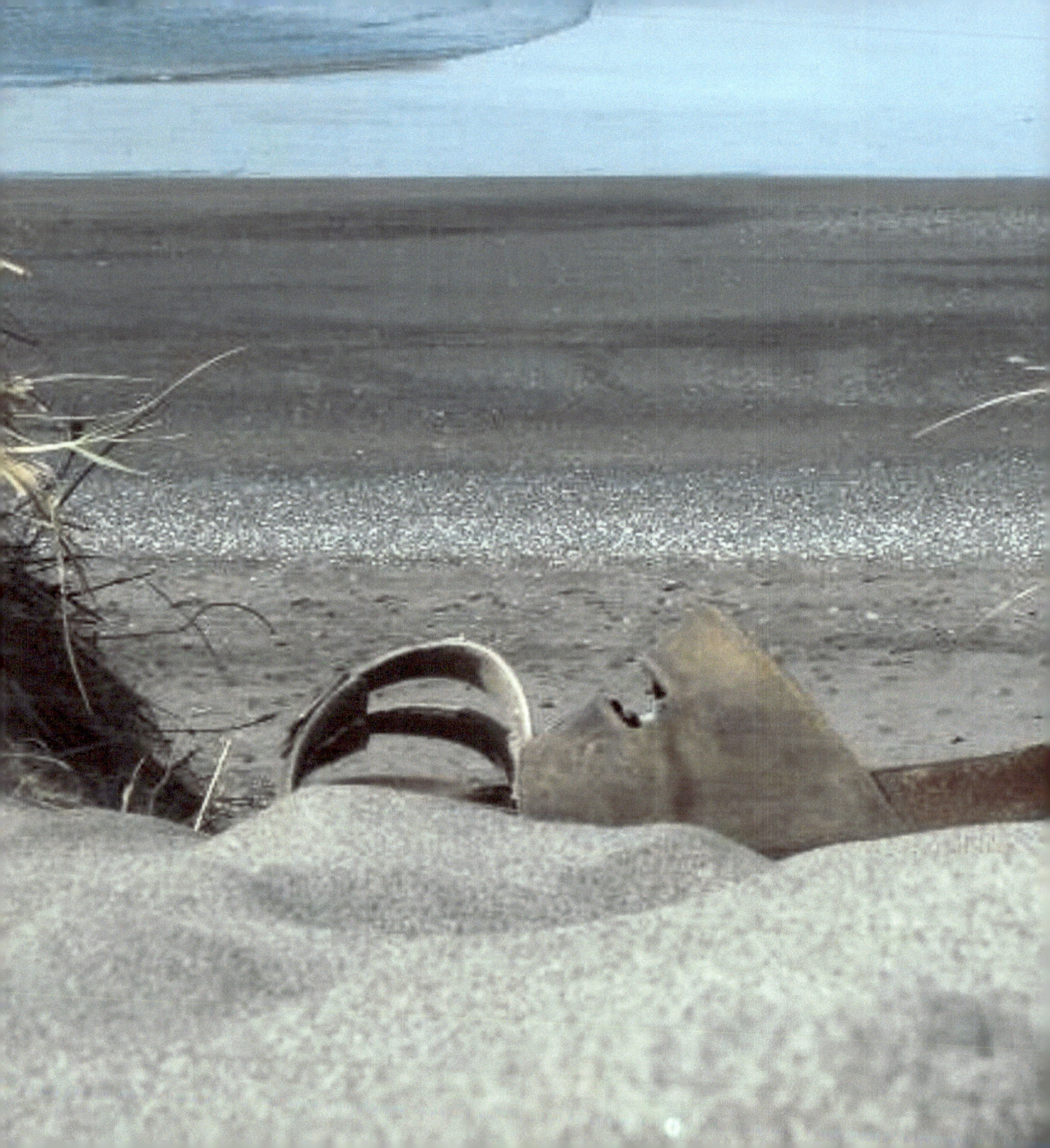

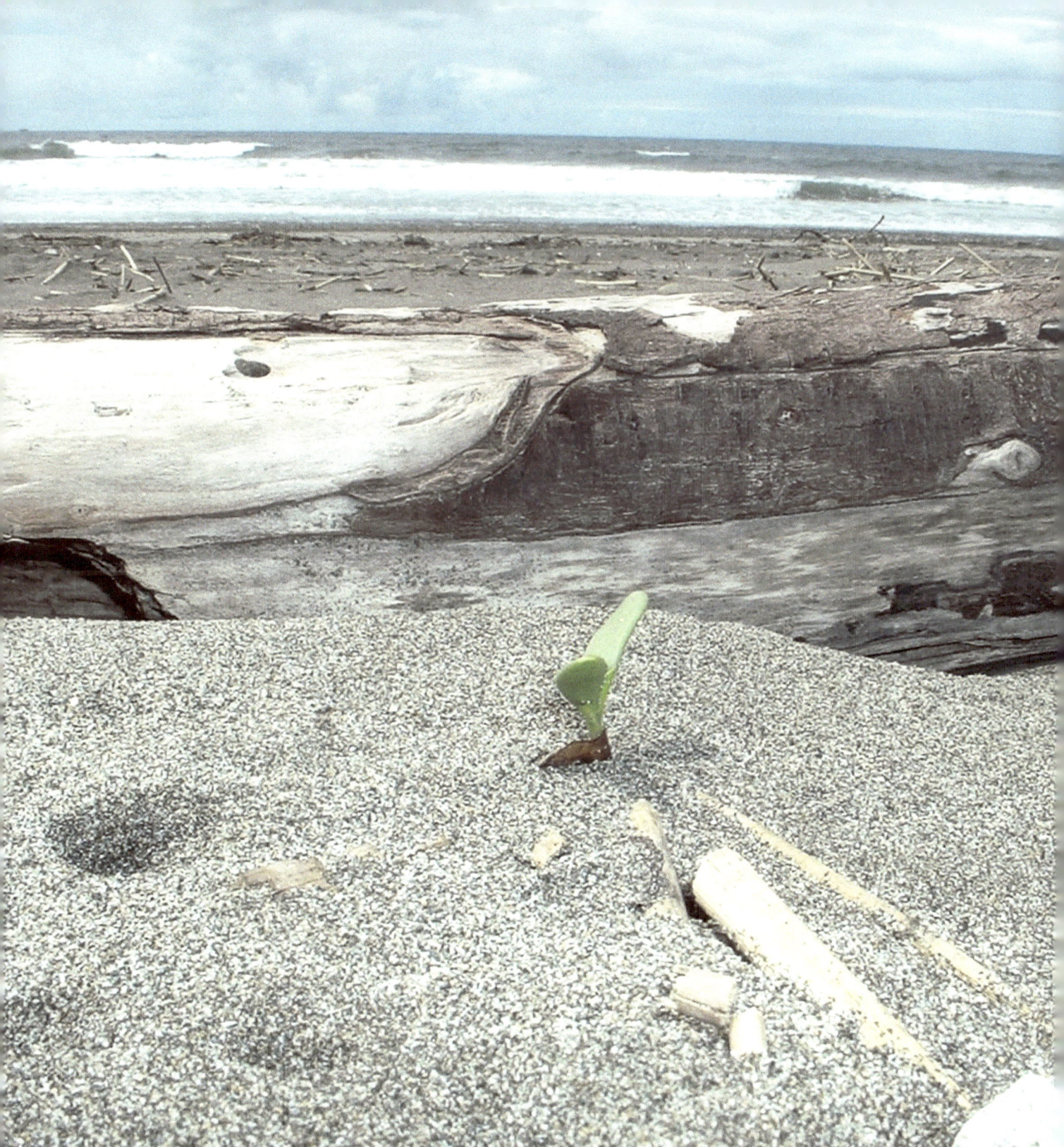

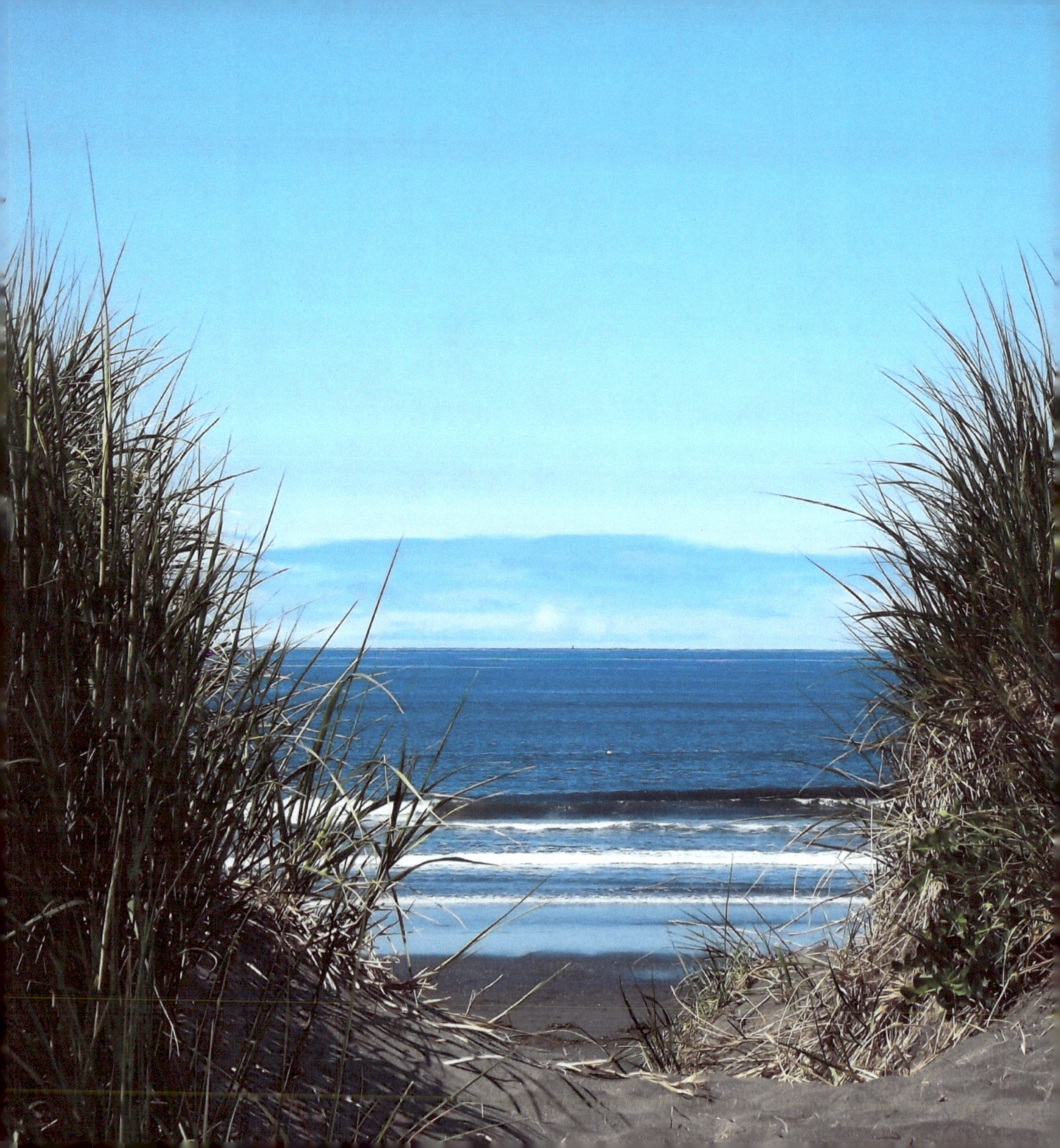

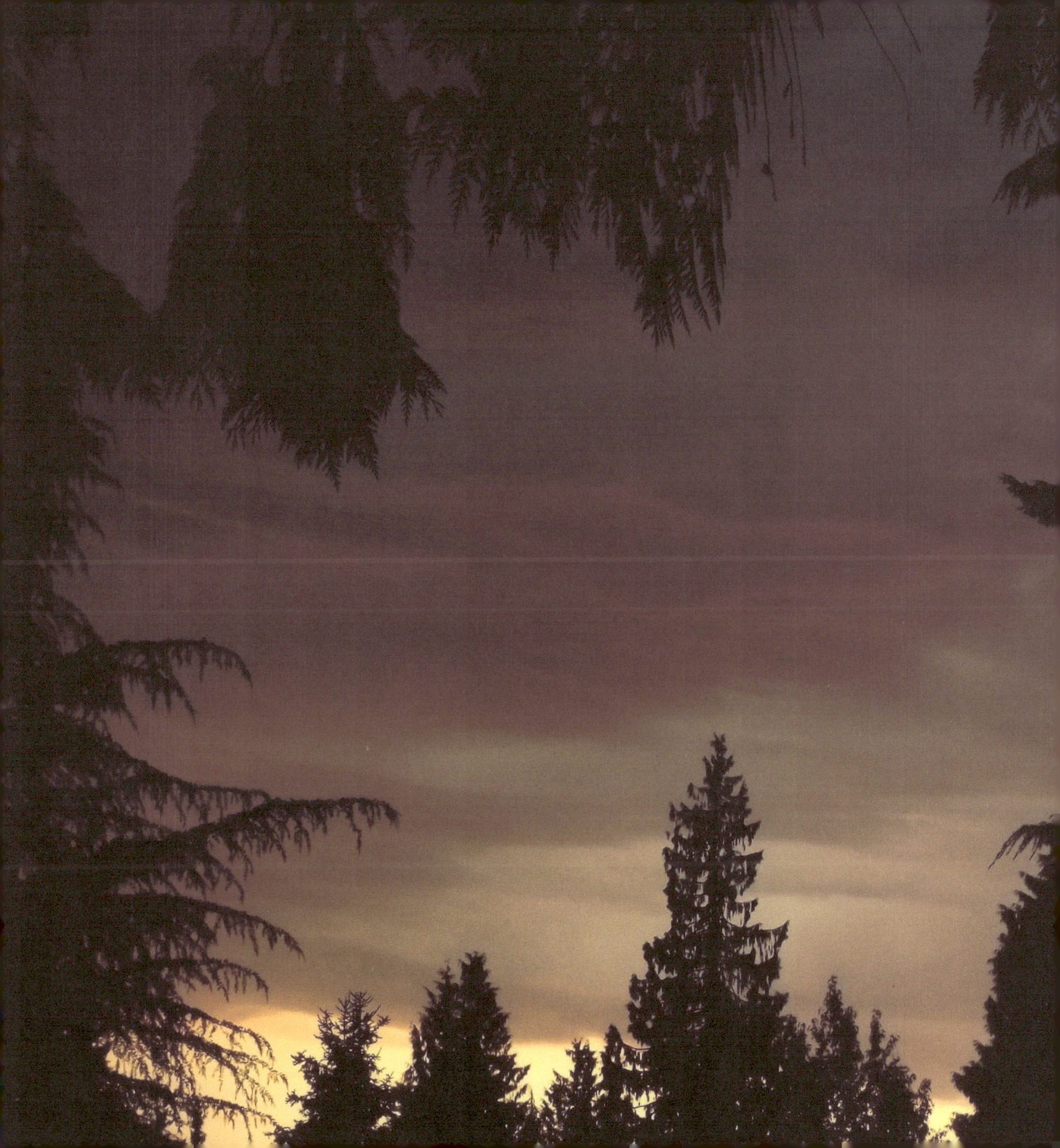

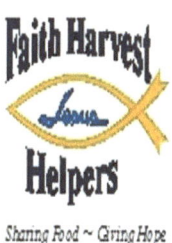

Faith Harvest Helpers

A Ministry of Youth with a Mission

Introducing Faith Harvest Helpers:

"To know God and to make Him known..." This is the motto and the guiding principle of Youth With A Mission International. Within this framework, Faith Harvest Helpers plays a vital role in *sharing food* and *giving hope*. Processing and distributing food as well as medical supplies and other essentials to needy people at home and worldwide, Faith Harvest Helpers is a vital and growing ministry centered around the principles and aspirations of Matthew 25:35... "For I was hungry and you gave me something to eat, I was thirsty and you gave me something to drink." It is this heart of servant-evangelism in meeting the needs of a hungry world –both physical and spiritual- which defines YWAM Faith Harvest Helpers.

Beginnings...

For over 20 years, members of Faith Harvest Helpers have made the yearly trek to YWAM Gleanings in California to help glean and process food which is sent to hungry people around the globe. During one of these trips, a vision was born to do something with surplus food in the Pacific Northwest. In 2006, Faith Harvest Helpers incorporated as a 501C3 and began processing surplus salmon from Washington State waters to share with those in need. In 2010, we grew to include a distribution center located in Yelm, Washington where fresh fruit, vegetables, bread, and dairy products could be distributed as well.

Growing...

Locally, approximately one million pounds of donated food is now processed and distributed by members and volunteers of Faith Harvest Helpers annually. This includes vegetables, bread, fruit, salmon, and dairy products. This is distributed by a small army of volunteers to benefit Pacific Northwest food banks and feeding programs.

Globally, we partner with a variety of other ministries to distribute non-perishable food, Christian literature, medical supplies, hygiene items, and other commodities with a message of hope.

Looking towards the future, we plan to acquire an approximately 45 acre farm property on the outskirts of Yelm to convert into a new and expanded ministry center. This will allow us to consolidate all ministry operations into one location, thus maximizing efficiency and good stewardship of resources. It will also vastly expand the opportunities for ministry and growth. Construction plans include warehouses, dorms, kitchens, a chapel, administrative offices, a training and discipleship facility, and large greenhouses. As plans unfold, we will be growing much of our own food to supplement donated items, utilizing state-of-the-art hydroponic technology. We will also develop a commercial cannery for fish and other commodities and continue in the role of "making disciples" through YWAM's Discipleship Training School.

Jump on board!

For information on how to volunteer, donate, or join an outreach, please contact paul@faithharvesthelpers.org.
You are also invited to visit our website: www.faithharvesthelpers.org.   Additional contact information is provided at the website.

Additional titles by Michael M. Middleton:

Modern Musings
The Great Deep, revised edition
Whispers of the Divine
Shadows and Substance
Sketches and Reflections

...And By Sharon Middleton:

On Winds of Change

www.ingramcontent.com/pod-product-compliance
Lightning Source LLC
Chambersburg PA
CBHW050811180526
45159CB00004B/1623